Relationship-Empowerment Parenting

Relationship-Empowerment Parenting

*Building Formative and Fulfilling
Relationships with Your Children*

Judy and Jack Balswick
and
Boni and Don Piper

Baker Books
A Division of Baker Book House Co
Grand Rapids, Michigan 49516

Published by Baker Books
a division of Baker Book House Company
P.O. Box 6287, Grand Rapids, MI 49516-6287
www.bakerbooks.com

Printed in the United States of America

Library of Congress Cataloging-in-Publication Data
Balswick, Judith K.
    Relationship-empowerment parenting : building family connections that last /
by Judy and Jack Balswick, and Boni and Don Piper.
        p.   cm.
    Includes bibliographical references.
    ISBN 0-8010-6402-3 (pbk.)
    1. Family—Religious life. 2. Parenting—Religious aspects—Christianity. 3. Interpersonal relations—Religious aspects—Christianity. 4. Children—Religious life. I. Balswick, Jack O. II. Piper, Boni. III. Piper, Don, 1943- IV. Title.
    BV4526.3 .B35 2003
    248.8′45—dc21   2002014967

To our children
Jacque, Jeff, and Joel
and
Aaron, Karlie, and Sarah

Contents

Preface

Has there ever been a task more demanding than that of being a parent? Can you think of any other job where you need to control an entire environment one year and take your hands off completely the next year? Has anything ever taken so much out of you, yet given you more joy? It's obvious from these questions that parenting is a lesson in paradox, a lesson in patience and perseverance, a lesson in learning to trust God.

We write this book to Christian parents who either are anticipating or are currently in the process of parenting. The uniqueness of this book is that we focus on four essential aspects of effective parenting that we find lacking in current parenting books. These four aspects are (1) a broad biblical model of the parenting relationship; (2) evidence from social science research that supports and confirms this biblical model; (3) practical insights and suggestions built on stories and experiences from all parenting life stages; and (4) wisdom that is based on accumulated expertise by the authors in their professional roles of pastor, sociologist, family therapist, and teacher of family ministry.

We are seasoned parents writing to those in the process of parenting. We've been through a lot and want to share what we have learned, now that our children are grown and out of the home. Through our personal and professional journeys, we've learned so much from our children. That is why we dedicate this book to them. They might not agree with everything we write here, but they can attest to the joys and the struggles, the ups and downs of relating as parents and children.

Besides the personal experience we bring to this task, we each have worked in professions that bring rich sources of knowledge to this topic. Judy, a licensed marriage and family therapist, teaches family therapy and supervision courses in the marital and family therapy program at Fuller Seminary. Jack teaches family ministry, child development, and cross-cultural courses in the same program. Jack and Judy have been able to coteach classes in gender and sexuality as well as present marriage and family enrichment workshops together. Boni, a full-time certified marital and family therapist in Seattle, is active in her church community. She has been a speaker in a variety of settings and has led marriage and family workshops with her husband. Don, a full-time pastor at Seattle Reformed Presbyterian Church, has served the church for over thirty years and has been on numerous boards in his denomination. In his role as pastor, he has counseled people from a biblical perspective. In addition, he has been a speaker at many family conferences and churches. These professional experiences have been invaluable in fashioning our ideas about the role and purpose of parenting in the life of a Christian.

While we bring accumulated wisdom through our training and experience, we remain humble about the task of writing a book on this topic. We (the Balswicks) remember the response of our sixteen-year-old daughter when we informed her we had been asked to give a parenting seminar at a local church. "What? You? You're going to tell parents how to raise children? Ha!" Now that our daughter has four sons of her own, we find it gratifying and a little amusing when she phones us for advice on parenting. What goes around comes around!

We certainly have made our share of mistakes as parents, and we don't claim to have all the answers. But we do offer an approach that we hope will empower parents. Our plan is not to present a recipe book on how to be "perfect parents." That would be absurd, because parenting is about relationships, not about rules and regulations that produce an end product. We believe that a solid understanding of developmental life stages (individual and family) provides a structure for viewing this parenting relationship, and research studies open our eyes to the important dimensions of parenting and how children are impacted by our approaches. But, more important, we look to Christ, the author and finisher of our faith, to live in and through us in our relationship with our children.

The goal in this book is to present comprehensive Christian principles of parenting. The idea is not to piece Bible verses together in order to form a model that fits certain cultural ideals. That is what we refer to as "strip-mining." Ignoring the historical and cultural context, the strip miner tears into the veins of Scripture, throws the unwanted elements aside, and emerges with selected golden nuggets of "truth." Too often, the search for God's truth about parenting ends up with principles that conform to the preconceived ideas of the miner. But basic parenting principles are gleaned from the whole of Scripture.

When we turn to Scripture, we find that our Heavenly Parent models relationship. Our strategy is to begin by examining the Creator God of the Old Testament, then to look to the incarnate Christ as he lived and moved and had his being among us, and finally to acknowledge the role of the Holy Spirit, who empowers and transforms us into godly parents.

Part 1 gives a foundation for the Relationship-Empowerment Parenting (REP) model. Chapter 1 begins with social science concepts of effective parenting. This knowledge is summarized in terms of four identifiable parenting styles—neglectful, permissive, authoritarian, and authoritative. An evaluation of each of these parenting styles is given in light of God as parent. Chapter 2 is a biblical and theological basis for parent/child relationships. We point out four key elements—God loves unconditionally rather than conditionally, God offers grace rather than shame, God's Spirit builds up rather than controls, and God knows us intimately and searches us out for intimate connection. Chapter 3 follows with a relationship-empowerment model of Christian parenting. Chapter 4 concludes this section with a focus on important dimensions of empowerment.

Part 2 deals with the major developmental stages in the parent/child relationship. Chapter 5 discusses the importance of establishing a secure, emotional attachment between parent and child. Much will be said about the necessity of establishing a solid foundation of love and trust. Chapter 6 focuses on the challenges brought about by the rapid changes that occur during the ages of six to twelve. We refer to this as the "golden age" of parenting, because children and parents typically are enthusiastic and joyful in their togetherness. Chapter 7 moves into the parenting of preteens. Issues of identity, character building, and self-esteem as well as social and interpersonal skills are especially important during this time in a child's life. Chapter 8 discusses the complex interaction between the typical strain of adolescence and the corresponding parental midlife struggles. Developing purpose and establishing meaning through relationships, work, faith, morality, and spirituality are important aspects in empowering teenagers. Chapter 9 brings out the mixed feelings that occur when children leave home. Chapter 10 deals with the complexity of relating with adult children.

In part 3 we conclude with parenting as a godly act. In chapter 11, we focus on Christian community. Some people claim that one's peer group matters more than one's parents when it comes to moral behavior and values. We certainly know that peer, media, and cultural influences have a direct impact on our children in these matters. But religious beliefs and the support of a strong faith community make a significant impact as well. In chapter 12 we look at parenting as a life-giving task. But it is more than this; it is a life-affirming privilege!

In appendix 1 you'll find the Relationship-Empowerment Parenting Inventory. This is a short questionnaire we have constructed to assist you in assessing yourself as a parent. You may want to complete this before you begin reading the book. However, your interpretation and understanding of the results will be made clear in chapters 1–3. Parts 1, 2, and 3 of the questionnaire correspond to the material discussed in chapters 1, 2, and 3 respectively.

The time spent writing this book was a special time for us as couples. Even though we've been friends for over thirty years (we met in Cyprus in 1972 when we were in the beginning stages of family life), it gave us a chance to deepen our friendship and engage in dialogue about our perspectives and differences. We are especially thankful to Jo Baskerville for giving us time at her wonderful cabin, Bali Hai, to do a good portion of the writing. Those freshly picked huckleberries on Swedish pancakes in the morning put us in the right frame of mind to accomplish our task!

We wish to thank Robert Hosack for encouraging us to go forward with this project and for his faithful efforts to see it through to completion. And to Kristin Kornoelje, who helped us correct, refine, and improve the manuscript, we are deeply grateful.

Our hope is that you will find what we've written to be anchored in the truth of Scripture, informed by the best social-science research, enlightened with humor and stories from friends, clients, and our families, sensitized by pastoral and therapeutic understanding, and tempered by our own personal experiences.

Part 1

Building a Biblical Foundation for the Parent/Child Relationship

1

Styles of Parenting in Contemporary Society

What's a Parent to Do?

Marianne went to the grocery store with her two preschool children. In the middle of the shopping trip, they "double-teamed" her and threw temper tantrums, causing her to leave her groceries and get out of there!

Beth's daughter Maia refuses to sleep in her own bed, so Beth lets Maia sleep with her most nights—so they both can get some rest.

Mark is disgusted with his preteen son Toby, who seems to have little interest in anything other than his computer. And who knows what he's doing on that thing! The whole parenting experience makes Mark uneasy, and other than yelling at Toby, he doesn't want to talk about it.

Charlene's sixth-grade daughter, Amber, refuses to do her homework unless she is rewarded with dessert. The school has called to tell Charlene and her husband that they must do something or Amber will not pass the grade.

Titus doesn't believe in letting his teens go out with friends on weekends. "It just disrupts the family life," he says. But now he's upset that they are disobeying him in ways he doesn't seem able to control.

Chari called her mom in tears because she had just screamed at Josh. "Am I a horrible mother? Have I damaged him?"

We live in an age of information. We attend seminars, watch videos, and read books to figure out how to survive this journey of parenting.

The books are varied, ranging from cookbook recipes (feeding schedules, manners at the table, dating rules) to more overarching models of psychology, attachment theory, child development theory, family life stages, and parenting training models. And between our own two families, we have read most of them!

So why is it so hard to be a parent today? Why is all this help not helping? Why are we still confused about what to do about temper tantrums, sleepless nights, and teen behaviors? After all, isn't good parenting something that comes naturally, and therefore should be easy? Didn't we all sit around as young adults, saying, "When I have kids, they'll never do this or that"? We sure did! All four of us, for example, came from basically good, though not perfect, families; we loved children and wanted to have children of our own. Now as we look back, we realize that raising our kids was probably the hardest and most challenging thing we have ever done.

Living in a postmodern society, where there is a plethora of perspectives and religious and personal values, makes parenting even more challenging. We're bombarded by secular culture and influenced by it whether we want to be or not. Redefinition of gender roles, living in a pluralistic society, glorification of youth culture, high divorce rates, new family forms (cohabitation, single parenthood, and reconstituted or blended homes), and geographic mobility are all part of our complex, rapidly changing world. Nothing stays still long enough for us to assess the impact it has on our families!

Perhaps it has never been easy to parent at any time in history or in any culture. It has always been an awesome responsibility for parents to build relationships and guide their children as they move from total dependency in the early stages, to mastering many developmental tasks, and finally to gaining a sense of self-direction that eventually leads to mutual interdependency. It has always been quite a journey for parents and children alike.

Sometimes We Feel like Such Failures

Most parents feel like failures at some point along the way. It's quite impossible to parent perfectly—we all fail in one way or another. And our insecurity about our parenting abilities often drives us to the experts and bullies us into searching for the exact formula that promises a successful product. We run to the nearest bookstore to search for the magic "how to" techniques that will guarantee success.

In our "cult of the expert" world, we as parents are prone to keep our eyes open and ears focused on the latest pearls of wisdom about the job.

We've been conditioned to doubt ourselves and question our sensibility. There are even books written to "dummies." Unfortunately, while these types of books may work for fixing cars or doing income taxes, when it comes to raising children, the stakes are much higher. Humans are much more complex than a machine or a project, so we should be skeptical of books giving black-and-white answers.

Relationships can't be prescribed through techniques. Rather, relationships grow out of an interaction between a unique parent and a unique child, under the unique circumstances of their lives. God created us to empower children through a relationship, not to make a product of them according to a preprogrammed packaged deal.

A Gift or a Product?

Henri Nouwen (1984) reminds us that a child is not a product but a gift. God doesn't ask us to make products so we can feel good about ourselves as parents. If we apply techniques in order to produce a certain kind of child, we'll be tempted to control and coerce our children into being what we want them to be. On the other hand, if we respond to our children as gifts from God and lay our defenses aside so we can interact creatively with them, this will bear fruit. And we will be extremely grateful for children who have become what God intended them to be— gifts beyond our wildest imaginations.

So we should affirm the seriousness of our calling and the responsibility of our leadership role as parents. We should open ourselves up to the joy and growth that happen when our parenting is a reflection of our relationship with God. And as we live out this call, we should rely on God's wisdom and truth, humbly respond to the grace of Christ when we fail, and look to the Holy Spirit for strength to go the extra mile.

We as authors encourage you to think critically about what we present in this book. In fact, we have some differences when it comes to certain preferences about parenting, both as couples and from mother/father perspectives. As you read, we'd like you to ask these questions:

- What is helpful and practical in this book for my family in my particular circumstances?
- In addition to the biblical principles, how do my personal experiences and family-of-origin dynamics impact my parenting?

We believe effective parenting has to do with discerning and incorporating what's in the best interest of each family. Hopefully we've dispelled the notion that, even though God is absolute and has given us solid principles to follow, there is one single method or technique that is correct when it comes to parenting. Rather, there are basic principles to guide us as we go along.

Relationship-Empowerment Parenting (REP Model)

The REP model (discussed in a later chapter) proposes guiding principles that will transform parent and child alike. The goal is not a finished product of our own making. Rather, the fruit of our labors is the transformation that emerges through the mutual relationship process. Our children will surprise us and sometimes disappoint us (as we surprise and disappoint them), but through it all, we should approach each other with a sense of awe about what God is doing in our lives.

While the Bible is not a parenting textbook, there are major biblical precepts that form the basis of our REP model. The four key principles (covenant, grace, empowerment, and intimacy) discussed in the next chapter are *rep*resentative of how God, our Heavenly Parent, relates to us as children.

The two essential dimensions of parenting, *relationship* (support) and *empowerment* (guidance), are the central focus of this book. We believe these concepts are clearly delineated in Scripture, as well as noted in social science research.

Now let's consider research findings related to these two dimensions, the parenting styles that emerge from them, and the impact they have on children. As you read through this next section, remember that people tend to parent as they were parented. So as you reflect on these styles of parenting, consider how you've been influenced by your own upbringing.

Parenting Preferences

An age-old debate centers on permissive parenting versus restrictive parenting. Permissive parents recognize the importance of warmth, affection, and emotional security, but downplay discipline. Restrictive parents, on the other hand, emphasize discipline, responsibility, and self-control, but pay less attention to emotional bonding and nurture.

In her comprehensive research, Baumrind (1996) identified three main parenting styles: authoritative, authoritarian, and permissive. We'll review the positive and negative aspects of the authoritarian and permissive styles as observed by Baumrind, and then present the authoritative style as the most complete and effective way to parent.

Authoritarian

Authoritarian parenting leads to obedience and high regard for authority in children. Studies indicate, however, that the kids from these homes are less able to think independently and take independent action. They also have only a moderate amount of social responsibility. Strict discipline fails to facilitate social competency, because the children don't internalize the values behind right behavior. In particular, coercive control (forcing children to do something against their will) was found to be debilitating. These children tend to be fearful, looking to others to define and determine their behaviors.

Coercive methods of control, whether physical or verbal, are intrusive and often arbitrarily based on the whims of the parent. Controlling behavior by withdrawing love may be effective, but it leaves children feeling insecure, anxious, and submissive simply out of a desire to be acceptable to their parents. While these methods may be effective in the short run, they are rarely successful in the long run, because the focus is on the external behavioral consequences rather than internalized values.

Permissive

Permissive parenting is based on the assumption that a child is born like a rosebud, needing only tender love and support to blossom into a beautiful flower. Children living under this philosophy tend to have everything given to them and done for them. Many become self-centered and self-indulgent and lack a social responsibility that takes them beyond themselves into concern for others.

Permissive parents believe that unstructured, free expression gives children the freedom to come to their own conclusions and discover their own values. But Baumrind (1996) found that insufficient guidance left children floundering. These kids have trouble figuring out rules for themselves and have to learn the hard way, through trial and error.

Although permissive parents may give plenty of acceptance and love, they fail to provide sufficient leadership. Their children develop a false perception of themselves at home but eventually find out that in real life, peers and teachers aren't quite as generous as their parents.

Authoritative

Authoritative parenting proved to be optimal, because it led to competent, responsible behavior in children. When there is both a high amount of proper discipline (guidance) and a high amount of relational support (emotional bonding, nurture), children do their best. The balance of relationship and empowerment (guidance) is most conducive to optimal growth and development. Children bask in the relationship qualities of love, acceptance, and affirmation but also are given confidence in their endeavors. Sufficient structure, wise guidance, clearly defined rules, firm limits, logical consequences, and direction empower them for competence, self-direction, and responsibility.

Two Leadership Approaches

Before we get bogged down with too much research, we'd like you to consider two approaches to parental leadership: social-emotional and instrumental. You'll notice how the social-emotional aspects comport with the relationship-empowerment dimensions just described. We'll briefly define the social-emotional and instrumental leadership approaches and then indicate four parenting styles that emerge when we intersect the social-emotional with the relationship-empowerment dimensions. Try to see where you fit in this scheme.

The social-emotional leader is interpersonally oriented and spends energy maintaining good relationships with children. This type of parent communicates well, pays attention to feelings, asks questions, and assists family members during conflicts and problem solving. Connecting at an emotional level is a high priority, and so is creating a safe atmosphere and relational quality in the home.

The instrumental leader is task and content oriented and focuses on things that need to be accomplished. This type of parent is good at organizing activities, setting goals, and keeping family members focused on accomplishing the goals. This parent is particularly good at inculcating beliefs, values, and attitudes, and teaching children what they must know and how they must behave in order to be members in good standing within the family or community.

While both types of leadership are necessary for the best possible parenting, these leadership skills are often not found within the same person. So, having briefly considered these relationship-empowerment dimensions, we will now present the social-emotional leadership approach with the four distinct categories within each cell.

Social-Emotional Styles

Four separate cells portraying the extremes emerge when we intersect the relationship-empowerment dimensions of social-emotional par-

Figure 1.1

Social-Emotional Parenting Styles

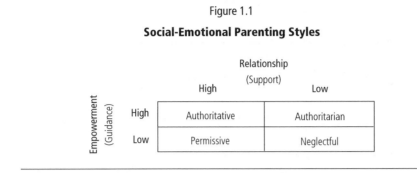

enting. The continuum from high to low relationship at the top of the chart refers to the basic support parents give their children. The continuum from high to low empowerment on the side of the chart refers to the parent's role in equipping and disciplining children. Each cell indicates one of the four social-emotional parenting styles. Parents can be either high or low in the amount of relational support they give their children and high or low in the empowering discipline they exercise over their children. By intersecting these two dimensions on the chart, we see the four parenting styles, empowering/authoritative, authoritarian, permissive, and neglectful. Next, we'll discuss and consider the implications of each style.

Authoritarian Style

Authoritarian-style parents are high on coercive control, strict about rules, and precise in discipline, but they are low on support. Their children tend to respect authority and readily obey, since disobedience leads to punishment, and punishment is to be avoided at all costs. They are kept in their place, are not included in family decisions, and are not to question their parents' authority. The home atmosphere is stilted, tense, and lacks spontaneity. In extreme cases, verbal and physical punishment is harsh and coercive, which leads to insecurity, fear, and anxiety in the children. There is not a loving relationship to counter the high priority on discipline and obedience.

Sometimes authoritarian parenting is the result of a cultural value. Eastern societies in particular permit mothers to be warm and nurturing with children, while fathers are granted the role of disciplinarian. Therefore, these fathers may stay more distant for fear of losing respect if they are too connected with their children. In other families, the mothers may be authoritarian, while the fathers are the benevolent ones. The split causes children to view one parent as the loving angel and the other as the feared ogre.

Look at this example of authoritarian parenting. An Asian-American youth from a Christian family was in therapy for "giving up" in school and being apathetic about life. When he first started therapy, he refused to talk, but after coming to trust his therapist, he began to express anger and fear about his father's harsh hand. He felt like he was a complete failure in his father's eyes and believed there was no way to please him.

When the parents came for therapy, the father admitted to hitting his son with his hand, as authoritarian parents are inclined to do. He didn't feel good about losing control and said, "I learned how to correct my son, but I don't know how to connect with him." The therapist asked the father to go into his son's room every night after his son was asleep and pray a prayer of blessing on him. The father did as requested, and it began to change his image into a father who blesses with his hand rather than punishes. This ability to develop a relational role as well as a disciplinary role opened up a new possibility between the father and son. The softening of discipline allowed the son to trust and be open to an emotional connection.

When each parent has balance between relational support and empowering discipline, the leadership is strong and harmonious. When parents learn to connect emotionally and develop assertive, firm leadership, they become more effective individually and together.

Permissive Style

Permissive-style parents have high relationship concern but take little leadership when it comes to correction or limit setting. As we've mentioned before, there is plenty of affirmation, warm fuzzies, and compliments in this style. The parents often idolize their children and believe they will find their way if left alone. This means the children have to make up their own rules, since the parents are reluctant to provide them. But trial and error is a hard way to learn, because children are bound to make many mistakes in the process of defining the limits.

Consider this example of permissive parenting. Sandy, a sixteen-year-old girl, came home later and later each night in an effort to get her parents to give her guidance. It wasn't good enough when her parents said they knew she would make the right decisions. She wanted specific input from them.

Most kids are like Sandy. They long for guidance. In fact, if they don't have guidelines or limits, they may feel their parents don't really care about them or their future. Support alone is not enough. Under the permissive philosophy, parents often fail to provide the needed empowerment.

Neglectful Style

Neglectful-style parents leave their children in the lurch. They don't provide relationship support *or* empowering discipline. Regardless of whether these parents are physically and/or psychologically unavailable due to mental illness, substance abuse, long work hours, etc., this style is grossly inadequate. Children have to compensate for lack of parenting out of default. They are expected to survive situations without many resources at their disposal. Mistakes are inevitable, and a neglectful situation often leaves children crushed, shamed, or confused much of the time.

The lack of supportive care takes a huge personal toll. In several excerpts from the novel *The Last Sin Eater* by Francine Rivers (1998), we can see how a young girl expresses her anguish at being neglected by a self-absorbed mother.

> I had been left alone with Mama's silence. No words passed between us. Not even a look. I was low and melancholy from abiding under the shadow of death. "Can I do anything for you, Mama?" She looked at me, and her pain was terrible to see . . . I thought then it would have been better had I died. (p. 17)

> I was alone. There was no one to love me back from the edge. (p. 20)

> Mama took one long look at me up and down, shut her eyes, and turned away. (p. 67)

Unfortunately, there are many neglected children in our world today. Some latchkey children, through no fault of their own, fall prey to this type of parenting. It certainly is true that a child can be orphaned in a war-torn country or orphaned in their suburban home.

As a result of neglect, children often feel unloved, unprotected, and vulnerable. When hopelessness sets in, it leads to depression, apathy, anxiety, and acting-out behavior. These children may look to peers or gangs—any authority that will provide clear-cut rules and direction—for a sense of belonging and meaning. After all, they may reason, it's better to follow an authoritative leader than live with the feeling that no one cares enough to discipline.

Authoritative (Empowerment) Style

In a well-documented study, Maccoby (1980) found that the balance of relationship support and empowering guidance contributes to social competence in children. She describes parents who empower their children as follows:

> They attempt to direct the child in a rational, issue-oriented manner; encourage verbal give and take; explain the reasons behind demands and discipline but also use power when necessary; expect the child to conform to adult requirements but also to be independent and self-directing; recognize the rights of both adults and children; set standards and enforce them firmly. These parents did not regard themselves as infallible but also did not base decisions primarily on the child's desires. (p. 376)

The balance of guidance and support, offered by both parents, leads to empowered, competent children. Maccoby found that children with this type of parent exhibit high self-confidence, achieve their academic capacity, have strong cognitive development, exercise creativity, have an internal locus of control, demonstrate moral behavior such as honesty and trustworthiness, and are competent in life skills. Children obviously thrive in such an environment.

Instrumental Parenting Approaches

Instrumental parenting can be considered along two separate dimensions, one involving action and the other involving content. Parents can be rated as high or low on the action and content scale.

High action means the parent is very involved in helping the child accomplish a task. For example, a father helps his daughter with a project for the school science fair. He goes with her to the store to purchase the needed equipment, he spends time each night helping build the structure, he goes over the research part to give suggestions and corrections. He is actively involved at many levels.

Parents can also be rated on whether they are high or low in content. A parent who is high in this dimension communicates through a rich elaboration of rules, beliefs, values, norms, ideology, etc. In contrast, being low in this dimension is characterized by the absence of verbal instruction or communication. In the case of the science project, the parent may participate through action but takes no interest in dialogue or asking provocative questions about what is being learned.

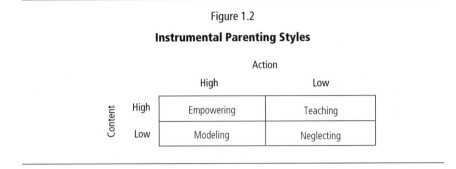

Figure 1.2

Instrumental Parenting Styles

		Action	
		High	Low
High		Empowering	Teaching
Low		Modeling	Neglecting

(Content is the vertical axis label with High and Low; Action is the horizontal axis label with High and Low.)

By placing these two dimensions into four cells, we represent four different kinds of instrumental parents. Let's look at the impact of each parenting modality.

Teacher

Some parents are great at explaining life to their children and are enthusiastic about all the things there are to learn about the world. This is the type of parent who delights in giving detailed descriptions to children at the zoo or museum. Yet teaching is only a partial form of parenting. While it is certainly important to instruct children about life and values, if there are contradictions in how parents live that life, children lose respect.

Adults are viewed as hypocrites when their strong teachings do not match their lifestyles. It's a difficult thing for children to swallow when their parents talk the talk but don't walk the walk. Though these parents may truly want to live up to the standards they teach, they often fail to do so. Even when it's not intentional, children feel deceived. Words begin to have an empty ring.

We knew of a father who could "teach" until the cows came home, yet his kids and their friends ridiculed him behind his back because he lived a life that was far removed from what he taught. And in a recent interview, a prominent movie star politely asked the interviewer not to take a picture of him smoking. He didn't want his kids to see it, because he has taught them that smoking is bad.

Modeler

The old adage that what children learn is caught and not taught applies here. Research shows that modeling is one of the most effective ways to inculcate values and desired behavior in children. Yet modeling is also only a partial form of parenting, because if parents are unable or unwilling to give reasons behind values, learning is limited. Kids are left to fill in the gaps and in the process may misunderstand, misinterpret, and be outright wrong in their conclusions. But when modeling is accompanied by thoughtful explanation, values are clearly grasped so they can become a congruent part of a child's life.

Modelers have some advantage over teachers, in that their behavior is congruent with their words. However, the lack of teaching the "whys" behind the expected behaviors leaves a gap that hinders a child's understanding.

Neglecter

The neglectful parent fails to take any leadership in the home. If both parents are ineffective or nonresponsive, it is disastrous to the children. Most likely, all family members are disconnected as each one tries to make it on his or her own.

It is painful to be ignored and avoided. And neglected children may lack even basic resources like food and shelter. All they can do is scramble on their own to make sense of their senseless world. God intended that children be protected and provided for by their parents. It is a sad state of affairs if we don't reach these parents and empower them to parent properly.

Empowerer

In the empowering role, parents influence through word *and* deed. Discipline, derived from the root word *disciple,* means one who leads or guides. The empowerer leads through teaching and modeling, words and action.

Empowerment happens in the context of the relationship. Parents are involved through their actions as well as through discussion and dialogue. They actively help their children master tasks, and they use instruction as an important resource in defining reasons and meaning behind the behavioral expectations.

An empowerer sets age-appropriate limits that are fair and flexible. They provide security through a stable and predictable environment, yet they adapt to the specific needs of the situation and development stage. They encourage autonomy and competence as well as connection and interdependence.

Parents Are Human Too!

Although we believe it's helpful to present these different styles of parenting, things are never quite as simple as these categories imply. The categories are hypothetical, and no parent operates exclusively in one extreme or the other. And it's not the parenting style or leadership role alone that determines effective parenting—it's the interactive impact of relationship and empowerment that matters.

Being invested in our children means we must pay attention to their emotional, cognitive, developmental, and spiritual growth. We take time to be "in tune" relationally as we monitor their activities. Managing schedules, peer associations, activities, and their physical whereabouts increases support as well as provides structure that empowers. Children are empowered through the relationship, and the relationship gives us the right to be influential in empowering ways.

Parenting is a transforming experience. We socialize children, but they also socialize us. Henry and Peterson (1995) found that social competence in children tends to elicit more competent parenting. Reciprocal socialization between parents and children serves as an active social agent of mutual influence.

Isn't this great? Isn't this what God intended by creating us as relational beings? In the parenting process, God changes, sanctifies, grows, and develops us. Wise parents follow in order to lead by being responsive and sensitive to their children.

And we also believe that it is God's plan that both a mother and a father raise children. Two are better than one, and parenting is a job for two parents. (Even if you are a single parent, one of the most important things you can do for your children is to share the parenting with someone else.) Relationship-empowerment is maximized when both parents are invested. While there may be differences in how mothers and fathers go about parenting, we believe that fathers are more competent today than in the past in nurturing activities such as holding, loving, feeding, vocalizing, and interacting. While mothers still tend to spend more time in caregiving activities, fathers are learning the joys of bonding with their children.

We believe children benefit greatly from a "double dose" of love and leadership. And the Bible clearly addresses mothers and fathers in the parenting role. In fact, nowhere does Scripture teach that mothering is more important than fathering.

We are not alone in this belief. Ehrensaft (1990) reported that coparented children have a more secure sense of basic trust; are more able to adapt to brief separations from the mother; have closer relationships to both mother and father; develop better social discrimination skills; display greater creativity and moral development; have less animosity toward the other gender; are better able to develop strong friendship bonds with opposite-gender children; and display fantasies of sustained connection with others.

Not surprising, it seems that sons especially benefit from shared parenting. Boys who have a strong bond with both their father and mother are more able to display empathy, affection, and nurturing behavior, are more likely to think highly of the way they were parented, and are more likely to state that they want to be a father when they grow up. Strong fathering has a positive effect on how boys develop relational skills. Boys who bond with their fathers are more nurturing and relational.

Girls who are coparented have a greater sense of self and personal boundaries. Also, when a father in particular takes an active interest in his daughter's achievements, she is more likely to succeed in her career goals. And mothers who model assertiveness and self-confidence, in addition to nurturing behaviors, give their daughters permission to set firm boundaries as well as make emotional connections with others.

In addition to being beneficial to children, coparenting can be beneficial to the parents as well. There is an accumulation of evidence demonstrating that a strong parental partnership enhances marriage. Trouble can brew when parents are not united in the task of parenting. If one parent is the harsh ogre, the other parent may take the opposite extreme and become the lenient, softhearted one. Instead of balancing each other, they let conflicts in style push them into even more polarized positions. In this case, children receive emotional support from one parent but receive very little from the other. Such splitting causes disruption in the marital relationship, and children inevitably get caught in side-taking tactics.

The complementary nature of shared parenting means children receive different strengths from each parent. When one parent needs relief, a second parent can be fully present and connected with the child. During a particular time of life, one parent may be called upon to be more involved on a day-to-day basis while the other takes special interest in organizing a weekend family event. One parent may do a great job helping with homework while the other is especially helpful with emotional issues. Dividing up parenting responsibility eases the burden, as long as both parents learn the needed skills such as nurturing and setting rules. Shared parenting is a rewarding investment that pays off in the end—it benefits fathers, mothers, children, and family life as a whole.

As we said before, shared parenting strengthens marriage. In an age when two-thirds of two-parent families are working outside the home, both spouses are needed within the home. Each parent must find a balance between work and family. One spouse may pull back from work commitments in order to increase time given to family life at a particular family stage. At another time, the other spouse may make adjustments by taking on more of the caregiving role.

When Sarah joined our (the Pipers) family, such adjustments had to be made. I (Boni) had already signed a part-time teaching contract when Don and I were told that an adoption did not look possible. But a few months later, Sarah arrived! Don was able to arrange his work schedule and be at home with Sarah three mornings a week while I was at school. He was able to make up the time by working some evenings, during which time I took charge of the children. The strong early attachment formed by Don and Sarah shows in their relationship to this day. Whatever the arrangement, both spouses benefit by equally respecting and honoring commitments to work and the home.

Take a look at the following list, which gives ideas on how to form a shared parenting model.

- Establish a close couple relationship
- Be flexible and adaptable to each life circumstance
- Agree on priorities
- Focus on the essentials
- Draw upon all the resources you can muster
- Be creative in finding solutions that work for you
- Relax "perfectionistic" household standards
- Keep from setting unrealistic expectations/goals
- Show appreciation for each other's efforts
- Don't polarize—find a middle ground
- Work as a unit and learn from each other
- Be part of a couples support group

We want to parent well. We want to balance relationship and empowerment roles and instrumental and social-emotional leadership. And we can benefit from studies on parenting because they help us be more thoughtful in raising our children. But we can only take this information so far as Scripture supports it. Having presented our relationship-empowerment parenting model (from this point on referred to as REP) and the research to support it, we will show in the next chapter an integrated model of Christian parenting.

Reflection Questions

1. Consider what it means to you that your child is a God-given gift. How will you parent differently than parents who think of children as an end product of their making? Do you see yourself as a gift in God's sight?
2. In what ways does the REP model *rep*resent God's way of parenting? List all the ways you believe God has built a relationship and guided you as his child.
3. Do you have a preference or tendency toward the social-emotional or instrumental parenting style? How can you develop a style that is more balanced?
4. If you are married, talk to your spouse about the strengths of coparenting and the areas where you aren't united in your parenting efforts. If you are single, list a person(s) you can go to for perspective and support.
5. If you have not done so already, complete part 1 of the Relationship-Empowerment Parenting Inventory given in Appendix 1.

2

A Biblical and Theological Basis

A basic premise of this book is that children are the Lord's good gift (Psalm 127). Contrary to what many might think, children are not merely a product of copulation with the purpose of propagating the species, nor even a necessary burden given to adults for the growth of God's kingdom. Rather, children are a gift from God, a heritage, and a reward. This truth from God lies at the heart of how we view our children and how we treat them.

As with all gifts from God, the gift of a child is accompanied by responsibilities. To understand the responsibilities that accompany children, we as parents must understand at least three things: the nature of the child, the relationship of the child to God, and the purpose of the child, which is to glorify and enjoy God forever. Once we understand these things, it is our responsibility and privilege to form a relationship that both guides and empowers children into fulfilling their purpose.

Created in God's Image

To understand the nature of the child, we go back to creation. In the Book of Genesis, we are told that God has made all humanity—men, women, boys, and girls—in his image: "So God created humankind in his image, in the image of God he created them, male and female he created them" (Gen. 1:27). Each human being, then, is in the image of God no matter what happens. Because we bear God's image, we must have a basic respect for each human being.

Though created in God's image, humanity did not remain in its created state. Our first parents, Adam and Eve, were without sin, placed in a beautiful garden and given dominion over the creation. In taking dominion, they were free to do anything except one thing: to eat of the tree of knowledge of good and evil. Adam and Eve had one simple directive that they chose not to obey. They intentionally reached beyond what was their rightful dominion and sought to usurp God's authority.

Through disobedience by our first parents, sin entered the world, bringing death and corrupting the image of God. The image was not destroyed, however. After the flood that wiped out all humanity except Noah and his family, God blessed Noah and said to him, "Whoever sheds the blood of a human, by a human shall that person's blood be shed" (Gen. 9:6). The reason for this command? "For in his own image God made humankind" (Gen. 9:6). Thus, the image of God, while corrupted, still exists in each human being. And each image of God commands respect.

Yet when our first parents fell into sin, it corrupted their nature, and they passed that corruption onto and through their children (Rom. 5:12–15). Children are not born blank slates. They are born prone to sin. We cannot assume that a child will choose good, even if the proper environment is provided. God's Word tells us, both in Psalm 14 and then in Romans 3, "There is no one who is righteous, not even one; there is no one who has understanding, there is no one who seeks God" (Rom. 3:10–11). Understanding that a child is both the image of God and is to be respected as such and corrupted by original sin and prone to do wrong is basic to parenting.

Prone to Sin

The bad news is that we are all prone to sin. But the good news that the Bible brings is that God has not left us in our sin. God made a covenant with the second person of the Trinity, who became Jesus. The covenant promise was that God would send a redeemer—Jesus, his own Son—to save us from our sins. He revealed this covenant to Adam and Eve in Genesis 3:15. According to this covenant, commonly referred to as the covenant of grace, humanity would be saved by God's grace rather than by anything humanity did or didn't do. Later, God made a covenant with Abraham, a covenant he called an everlasting covenant: "I will establish my covenant between me and you, and your offspring after you throughout their generations, for an everlasting covenant, to be God to you and to your offspring after you" (Gen. 17:7). The covenant God made with Abraham was essentially a promise by God that he would be God to Abraham and to his children. God would save him and his children by grace, and they were to respond in obedience.

It is important to understand that the covenant was not only with Abraham but also with his children. It was renewed with Abraham's son Isaac (Gen. 26:3–4), with Isaac's son Jacob (Gen. 28:13–15), and with Jacob's children, the whole nation of Israel (Deut. 5:1–6). From the beginning, children were always seen as an integral part of the covenant. When it was reviewed just before Israel entered the Promised Land, God said, "Assemble the people—men, women, and children, as well as the aliens residing in your towns—so that they may hear and learn to fear the LORD your God and to observe diligently all the words of this law, and so that their children, who have not known it, may hear and learn to fear the LORD your God, as long as you live in the land that you are crossing over the Jordan to possess" (Deut. 31:12–13).

Many years later, Jesus came and fulfilled the covenant. He died for his people's sin. He redeemed them according to the promises made to Adam and Eve and, more specifically, to Abraham and Sarah, Isaac and Rebekah, and Jacob and Rachel. But we may wonder if the covenant is still in effect. And are children a part of it?

Jesus *fulfilled* the covenant. He did not *nullify* it. And all who trust in Jesus Christ are recipients of it. Paul writes to the Galatians:

> For in Christ Jesus you are all children of God through faith. As many of you as were baptized into Christ have clothed yourselves with Christ. There is no longer Jew or Greek, there is no longer slave or free, there is no longer male and female; for all of you are one in Christ Jesus. And if you belong to Christ, then you are Abraham's offspring, heirs according to the promise.
>
> Galatians 3:26–29

Male and female are now heirs in the way only sons could be before. This is certainly true of adults who are trusting in Jesus, but what about their children?

In Acts 2, Peter is preaching the gospel to a large crowd gathered in Jerusalem to celebrate Pentecost. After hearing the gospel, the people ask Peter, "What shall we do?" Peter responds: "Repent, and be baptized every one of you in the name of Jesus Christ so that your sins may be forgiven; and you will receive the gift of the Holy Spirit. For *the promise is for you, for your children,* and for all who are far away, everyone whom the Lord our God calls to him" (Acts 2:38–39, italics added).

So while children have a nature corrupted by original sin, the children of Christian parents also have a special relationship with God. He made a promise to parents and their children to be their God, and he calls them to respond by trusting in Jesus Christ for forgiveness of their sins.

Purpose

Children of believers are related to God by covenant, and in turn they are gifts from God to parents. But what is their purpose? Why do they come into the world? Why did God create humanity?

Children, all of us, come into the world with the basic purpose of glorifying God and enjoying him forever (Westminster Catechism). We are to "strive first for the kingdom of God and his righteousness" (Matt. 6:33). The Bible, the Word of God, teaches us how to do this. Consequently, parents must acquaint their children with the Word of God, where they find who God is, who they are, and what their relationship to God and his creation is.

God tells parents in Deuteronomy 6:6–7: "Keep these words that I am commanding you today in your heart. Recite them to your children and talk about them when you are at home and when you are away, when you lie down and when you rise." Notice when we are to be explaining God's Word to our children—when we sit at home, when we walk along the road, when we lie down, and when we get up. In other words, this is a full-time job! We also are to answer questions our children may have about God and his world. In Deuteronomy 6:20–21, we're told that when our children ask the meaning of God's laws, we should be ready to tell them.

As parents, we are the ones ultimately responsible for our children's educations. We are responsible for telling them who they are as God's covenant children and what their relationship is to God. We need to make sure they are told the eternal truths, and we should empower them to be and do what God has called them to. From the time our children are born, we must read to them from God's Word. We need to pray with them and teach them to pray. We should make sure they worship with the rest of God's covenant people. And we must nurture them in such a way that they can take their place in God's community.

"Abba! Father!"

Children learn of God not only from what we say but also by experiencing who God is through us. Over and over again throughout Scripture, God uses the figure of a parent as a figure of himself. God as parent becomes our model. When we pray, Jesus tells us to call God "our father" (Matt. 6:9). The apostle Paul tells us in Romans 8:15, "For you did not receive a spirit of slavery to fall back into fear, but you have received a spirit of adoption. When we cry, 'Abba! Father!' it is that very Spirit bearing witness with our spirit that we are children of God."

Abba is an intimate Aramaic term meaning something similar to *daddy*. When we trust in Jesus, we become God's covenant children, adopted into his family. With that adoption, we have the rights of the heirs of God.

God portrays himself as a benevolent parent, primarily to help us understand him and our relationship to him. For instance, in Psalm 103:13 we read of how God forgives our sins: "As a father has compassion for his children, so the LORD has compassion for those who fear him." In Isaiah, God compares our relationship to a mother and child. "Can a woman forget her nursing child, or show no compassion for the child of her womb? Even these may forget, yet I will not forget you. See, I have inscribed you on the palms of my hands" (Isa. 49:15–16). Jesus, mourning for Jerusalem, says, "I have longed to gather your children together as a hen gathers her chicks under her wings" (Matt. 23:37). God gives us a picture of a parent willing to do what is necessary to bring children to salvation.

The Book of Hosea portrays God as a parent who pursues his children with an everlasting covenant love. Listen to his anguish and love when Israel turns away from him:

> When Israel was a child, I loved him
> and out of Egypt I called my son.
> The more I called Israel,
> the further they went from me.
> They sacrificed to the Baals
> and they burned incense to images.
> It was I who taught Ephraim to walk,
> taking them by the arms;
> but they did not realize
> it was I who healed them.
> I led them with cords of human kindness,
> with ties of love;
> I lifted the yoke from their neck
> and bent down to feed them . . .
> How can I give you up, Ephraim?
> How can I hand you over, Israel? . . .
> My heart is changed within me;
> all my compassion is aroused.
> I will not carry out my fierce anger,
> nor will I turn and devastate Ephraim.
> For I am God, and not man—
> the Holy One among you.
> I will not come in wrath.

Hosea 11:1–4, 8–9

And Jesus himself, in conveying God's compassion and goodness, uses the figure of a parent when he says, "Is there anyone among you who, if your child asks for bread, will give a stone? Or if the child asks for a fish, will give a snake? If you then, who are evil, know how to give good gifts to your children, how much more will your Father in heaven give good things to those who ask him!" (Matt. 7:9–11).

The Compassionate Parent

Probably the most well-known picture of God is found in the parable of the prodigal son. A better title of that parable might be "The Compassionate Father," because the purpose of the parable is not so much to teach us of the son but to teach us of the compassion and mercy of God.

While God's primary purpose in this biblical comparison is to teach us about himself by using the image of a good father, we also can use the parable to see what a parent should be like. The principle governing God's actions toward us, and which must govern our actions as parents toward our children, is grace—the grace found in God's everlasting covenant and that expresses itself in unconditional love. In the parable of the compassionate father, God's unconditional love is shown in a variety of ways, and through this example we can discover how we should respond to our own children in difficult circumstances.

By reading this story, we learn how to respond when a child insists on making a bad choice. In the parable, the son asks for his share of the inheritance while the father is still living. He can't wait until his father dies! The father is hurt and shamed before the whole community, yet he doesn't vent his feelings. In love, he endures the shame. When our children shame us, we shouldn't lash out. When they are older and make a choice we know to be destructive, we shouldn't interfere with threats of retaliation or give ultimatums.

By reading this story, we also can learn of perseverance in love. The father waited patiently, but no doubt in agony, for his son to return. Then he humiliated himself by running through the streets of the village to save his son the embarrassment and shame of trudging through the village. The son repented of his action and was ready to be a hired hand in his father's household, but the father didn't even let him get the offer out. He forgave his son immediately and restored him to his place of honor.

As God treats us this way, with such unconditional love, surely it is also the way we are to treat our own children. Just as the father in the parable did not stand with arms folded, waiting for his child to prove himself and work his way back into the family, so we must be ready to act in grace and forgive our repentant children.

Promise and Deliverance

Promise and deliverance are the major themes of Scripture. They are God's covenantal commitment to his people. God promises that he will be our God, and he sent Jesus to deliver us. Taken as a whole, the Bible proclaims a secure love and grace that will not let us go. In Romans 8 we see that once we are God's children, nothing can separate us from him. We may still be disciplined. But discipline is a mark of love.

Covenant commitment is both an action and an attitude. It's difficult to be steadfast and to make the best interests of others a priority. Yet actions of support and discipline are woven together throughout our life in Christ. And parents are challenged with the awesome responsibility of leading, teaching, loving, modeling, and disciplining their children in the same way God does. Any effective relationship requires time, energy, effort, humility, firmness, tenderness, and empathy.

Elements in a Theology of Parent/Child Relationships

With this theological foundation in place, we suggest that parent/child relationships can be best understood in the four sequential, circular relationship concepts of covenant, grace, empowerment, and intimacy. The logical beginning point of the parent/child relationship is covenant love. Unconditional commitment by the parents to the children is critical to the children's development. Knowledge that nothing can ever separate them from the love of their parents provides assurance that builds confidence. What develops out of the security provided by covenant love is grace. And in an atmosphere of acceptance and forgiveness, empowerment occurs. Empowerment comes through equipping, guiding, directing, affirming, encouraging, supporting, in order to help children develop their potential. When children are empowered, they have a great capacity to develop mutual intimacy with their parents. Mutual intimacy is grounded in love, grace, and empowerment, and leads back to a deeper level of covenant commitment. It is a circle of love that cycles inward and outward and penetrates relationships inside and outside the family.

The sequential change in Figure 2.1 is shown by a spiraling inward in order to represent the potential for the parent/child relationship to grow into even deeper levels of mutual commitment, grace, empowerment, and intimacy. The relationship between a parent and infant child

Figure 2.1

A Theology of Parent/Child Relationships

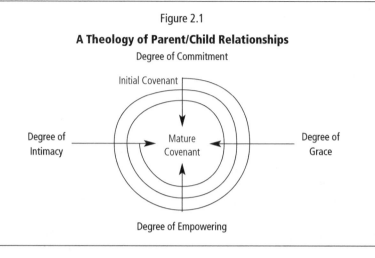

begins as a unilateral (one-way) love commitment. As the parent lives out that commitment, the relationship has the potential to grow into a bilateral (two-way) love commitment. This is an ongoing process of mutual growth and satisfaction.

It should be noted that we are not proposing a parent/child relationship that leads to exclusivity. On the contrary, it is the depth of the relationship between parent and child that is the impetus for reaching out to others in the family, community, and world. In addition, we believe that the covenant community of faith—the church—serves the family and is its best resource.

It should also be noted that growth in the parent/child relationship can be blocked or constrained at any point in the cycle. For example, if parents or children are unable or unwilling to reciprocate or respond, growth in the relationship can come to a standstill. Because relationships are dynamic, being stuck limits the progress and potential for growth. In this stagnant place, the tendency is to fixate on contract rather than covenant, law rather than grace, possessive power rather than empowerment, and personal distance rather than intimacy.

The four elements of growth in the parent/child relationship are considered as separate sequential stages for analytic purposes only. In practice, covenant, grace, empowerment, and intimacy are experienced simultaneously. Thus, the futility of pressing the suggested logical sequence into a strict linear model is evident. However, considering each separate dimension in depth will provide a better understanding of each of these four elements in the parent/child relationship.

We also recognize that although we are created in the image of God, we are fallen creatures who fail in all aspects of relationship with God and others. There is a sense in which no person can ever make a covenant in a relationship the way Almighty God covenants with us. Nor will any of us be able to live out the acceptance and forgiveness aspects of grace in the complete way Jesus does. Our empowering attempts will sometimes resemble possessive power—it is the Holy Spirit that truly empowers. And finally, our attempts at intimacy will pale when compared to God's knowing and caring. Yet we are hopeful, because God has invited us to develop a deep spiritual connection so we can have the heart and mind of Christ in us.

Covenant: To Love and Be Loved

We have already noted the place of the covenant in the theology of redemption. Now we will consider it in detail as it relates to how we deal with our children. You may remember that God makes a covenant in Genesis 17:1–7, in which a promise is extended to Abraham:

> "I am God Almighty; walk before me, and be blameless. And I will make my covenant between me and you, and will make you exceedingly numerous." Then Abram fell on his face; and God said to him, "As for me, this is my covenant with you: You shall be the ancestor of a multitude of nations. . . . I will establish my covenant between me and you, and your offspring after you throughout their generations, for an everlasting covenant, to be God to you and to your offspring after you."

Abraham's participation in the covenant is given in Genesis 17:9: "God said to Abraham, 'As for you, you shall keep my covenant, you and your offspring after you throughout their generations.'"

So what do we learn of parenting from this account? First, we see that God was not offering Abraham any choice in the matter. That is, God did not say to Abraham, "I would like to be your God. What do you think of the idea? I'll do it if it's what you want." Instead, the establishment of the covenant was based entirely on God's own action. His offer was not contractual; it was not based on Abraham's keeping his end of the bargain. God imposed the covenant, he made a promise, and that was that.

Second, we see that God expected a response from Abraham. Abraham was to obey God and circumcise those in his family as a sign of the covenant. Did this make God's covenant conditional? Was God "free" to retract the promise if Abraham or his children disobeyed? The answer is a resounding "No!" The covenant God made was "an everlasting covenant," regardless of what Abraham did.

Third, we see that while the potential *material* blessings provided by the covenant were conditional—Israel prospered as they walked in obedience to God and suffered when they disobeyed God—the continuation of God's love was not conditional. He was to be faithful to them regardless of their faithlessness.

Fourth, it is important to note that the covenant was made not just with Abraham but with his family as well. The covenant was "everlasting" in that it extended to generation after generation. Such is further evidence of the unconditional nature of the covenant.

The biblical account of how God deals with his covenant people is analogous to the unconditional love parents are to have for their children. A reading of the Old Testament Scriptures reveals the cycle of Israel turning away from God time after time—they get into difficulty, God forgives and saves them, and they are reconciled into the parent/child relationship.

We can also see the life of Jesus as the supreme expression of unconditional love. It is significant that Jesus tells the story of the prodigal son in response to those who were criticizing him for welcoming and eating with sinners. Just as the compassionate father in the story welcomed his wayward son home with open arms, Jesus demonstrated his unconditional love to a disobedient people. The unconditional nature of God's love is perhaps most clearly expressed in 1 John 4:19, "We love because he first loved us," and 1 John 4:10, "In this is love, not that we loved God but that he loved us."

While God's love is unconditional, should there be reciprocity? Yes, of course. The desire and the expectation of God is that, in response to his love and deliverance, we will in turn love him. While his commitment is unconditional, he expects that eventually his love will be reciprocated.

Figure 2.2 illustrates the potential types of parent/child commitments, where the relationship is either unilateral (one way) or bilateral (two way) in combination with it being either conditional or unconditional. In a parental context, when a child is born, the parents make an unconditional commitment of love to that child. The infant is unable at that time in life to make a reciprocal commitment. This is represented in the upper right cell as an *initial covenant* commitment. However, as the child matures, he or she may desire that the unilateral relationship develop into a mutual relationship, or what we have labeled as a *mature covenant* in the bottom right cell of Figure 2.2.

True reciprocity occurs when parents themselves age and become socially, emotionally, and physically more dependent on their adult chil-

Figure 2.2

Types of Commitment in Family Relationships

	Conditional	Unconditional
Unilateral	Open Relationship	Initial Covenant
Bilateral	Contract Relationship	Mature Covenant

dren. Here, in an equally mature and adult bilateral commitment, recip-rocal and unconditional love is especially rewarding.

Cells in the first column of Figure 2.2 represent two types of condi-tional parent/child relationships. In the *open relationship*, the parent is conditionally committed to the parenting role only as long as satisfac-tion is derived from the relationship. Such parents, and children, if they are old enough to be committed to the relationship, understand that when their needs are not being met in the relationship, they are free to end it. In his book *Fatherless America* (1995), David Blankenshorn doc-uments that an epidemic proportion of American fathers come close to exemplifying this type of parental commitment.

The *contract relationship* represented in the bottom left cell is condi-tional, but it is based upon the agreement that the relationship will con-tinue if both parent and child fulfill the agreed-upon conditions in the relationship. The relationship is a quid pro quo arrangement, in which both parent and child consider they have fulfilled the contract if they get about as much, or anticipate getting about as much, as they give in the relationship.

In reality, much of the daily routine in family life is lived out accord-ing to informal contractual agreements. Those who are advocates of relationships based on covenant do recognize the importance of mutual satisfaction and fairness promoted in these contractual agreements, but they also acknowledge that family relationships based on contract alone will forego the extraordinary dimensions of covenant love.

Grace: To Forgive and Be Forgiven

We indicated previously that we have separated the four elements of our theology of parent/child relationships for analytical purposes only. This is especially true in distinguishing between covenant and grace. By its very nature, covenant *is* grace. From a human perspective, the unconditional love of God makes no sense except as it is offered in grace. Grace is truly a relational word; one is called to share in a gracious relationship with God.

The incarnation is the supreme act of God's grace to humankind. Christ came in human form to reconcile the world to God. The love and forgiveness in the life, death, resurrection, and ascension of Jesus Christ is the basis for human love and forgiveness. We can forgive others as we have been forgiven, and the love of God within makes it possible for us to love others in the same unconditional way.

God designed the parent/child relationship to be lived out in the same way our relationship to God is lived out—in the atmosphere of grace, not law. In saying this, we the authors hasten to explain, as Paul did to the Roman church, that God's law is "holy, and the commandment is holy and just and good" (Rom. 7:12). If God's law is righteous and good, what do we mean when we say that the parent/child relationship should exist in an atmosphere of grace, not law? Do we mean that God's law has no relevance, or that there are no rules in the family? Not at all! Rather, we mean that neither children nor parents should ever be under the impression that love is conditioned on the children's strict obedience to law. Family life based on contract leads to an atmosphere in which law reigns and grace is absent; family life based on covenant leads to an atmosphere of grace and forgiveness. At both the individual and family level, grace provides freedom from the burden of living under legalism and gives a motive for family members to act responsibly out of love and consideration for one another.

We implied above that there is a place for law in the parent/child relationship. But just what is that place? Of course, we don't wish to imply that when grace is present, there is no need for law. So our answer to this question is what the apostle Paul wrote in his letter to the Roman church in chapter 10, verse 4: "Christ is the end of the law so that there may be righteousness for everyone who believes."

The law, far from being bad, points the way to God. However, since no human being is perfect, only Christ can fulfill the law. It is due to his perfection and righteousness that every believer is righteous—not because we haven't sinned but because Christ's righteousness is imputed to us. In other words, our salvation is not dependent on keeping the law but on Christ's faithfulness to the law. We then receive our salvation through our faith in him.

Much the same can be said for parent/child relationships. Through reading the Scripture, we can know something of God's ideal, but none of us can measure up to that ideal. In a family based on law, perfection is demanded. Rules and regulations are set up to govern relationships.

This kind of pressure adds guilt to the failure that is inevitable in such a family situation.

Although the covenant of grace rules out law as a basis for parent/child relationships, family members living in grace accept law in the form of patterns, order, and responsibility. God's law is good, and it is what we should strive for. In reality, much of our daily routine of family life must be lived according to agreed-upon rules. But grace recognizes that order and regularity are present for the sake of the enhancement of each family member and not as a means of repressing any part of the family.

Empowerment: To Serve and Be Served

The most common and conventional definition of power is the ability to influence another person. When using power, people try to decrease rather than increase the power of those they are trying to influence.

Empowerment is a biblical model that is completely contrary to the common concept of power. It can be defined as the attempt to establish power in another person. But empowerment is not merely yielding to the wishes of another person, nor does it necessarily involve giving up one's own power to someone else. Rather, empowerment is the active, intentional process of enabling the acquisition of power in another person. The person who is empowered has gained power because of the encouraging behavior of the other.

If covenant is the love commitment and grace is the underlying atmosphere of acceptance, then empowering is the action of God in our lives, and it is seen in the life of Jesus. Jesus said: "I came that they may have life, and have it abundantly" (John 10:10). The apostle John says of Jesus: "But as many as received him, to them gave he power to become the children of God, even to them that believe on his name: Which were born, not of blood, nor of the will of the flesh, nor of the will of man, but of God" (John 1:12–13). The Greek word translated "power" may also be translated "right" or "authority." Even if "right" or "authority" is the translation used, "authority" implies power, power that a true child of God would rightly have. And the power comes, as the verses tell us, not by physical or conventional means but from God. In Ephesians 3:16, the apostle Paul prays this for the people of God: "I pray that, according to the riches of his glory, he may grant that you may be strengthened in your inner being with power through his Spirit, and that Christ may dwell in your hearts through faith, as you are being rooted and grounded in love." This is the supreme example of human empowerment. After all, in the beginning, God gave authority to his children to rule over creation. And through the Holy Spirit, each child of God is empowered to do just that.

And how do children of God exert their authority as heirs? How does Jesus use his power? Jesus redefined the understanding of power by his teaching and by relating to others as a servant. He rejected the use of power to control others and instead affirmed the use of power to serve others, to lift up the fallen, to forgive the guilty, to encourage responsibility and maturity in the weak, and to give power to the powerless.

In a very real sense, empowerment is love in action—it is the loving and empowering seen in Jesus Christ that we as parents need to emulate. The practice of empowerment in parenting could revolutionize our view of authority in families. We the authors believe that authority in marriage is currently a controversial issue largely because people have accepted a secular view of the use of power. Many believe that power is a commodity of limited supply and is in the hands of the person who possesses the most resources. The good news for Christians is that, according to Scripture, the power of God is available to God's children in unlimited amounts! Paul writes to the church: "Now to him who by the power at work within us is able to accomplish abundantly far more than all we can ask or imagine . . ." (Eph. 3:20).

Much traditional thinking about parent/child relationships is based on the false assumption that power is in limited supply. Thus, parents often fear that as children grow older and gain more power, this automatically reduces parental power. But an empowerment approach to parenting begins by distinguishing between power and authority. In a biblical sense, parental authority is an ascribed power. The Greek word translated into English as "authority" is *exousia*. *Exousia* literally means "out of being." The authority given by God to parents is an influence that is not dependent on any achieved skill or characteristic but rather comes from "being" a parent.

We must take this role seriously and neither neglect it nor abuse it. This means we must take responsibility to care for our children's physical, social, psychological, and spiritual development. The process of empowering children certainly does not mean that we will be depleted or drained of power as we parent. Rather, successful parenting has to do with children gaining personal power and parents retaining personal power throughout the parenting process.

Empowerment in a family is the process of helping children recognize the gifts, strengths, and potential God has given them, as well as encouraging and guiding the development of these qualities to be used for God's glory. It is the affirmation of the children's ability to learn and grow and become all that God wants them to be. It may require times in which the empowerer steps back, allowing the child to learn by doing.

It is important that the one who empowers respects the uniqueness of each child's capacity to be competent.

All of us know how tempting it is to keep our children dependent. In fact, it is often rationalized as something that is done for the children's good. Most often, however, it is our own fear that keeps them in a dependent position. But when empowerment is the ultimate goal, we can release our children from parental control into self-control. Of course, mistakes will be made in the process of trying out new "wings" of responsibility, and this is the biggest test for those parents who don't want to let go. What we should remember is that the key to parental authority lies not in external control but in helping children develop an internal control that is well integrated into their spiritual lives and personality.

Taking a positive view of leadership means that we may need to rethink the idea of power. But security lies in the fact that we have a powerful personal connection with our children. And out of that relationship our children gain competence, mastery, and a desire to be responsible.

Intimacy: To Know and Be Known

Our Christian faith is distinct from Eastern religions in that God has broken into human history in order to be personally related to us. One of the major themes running through the Bible is that God knows us, even in our inmost being, and desires to be known by us. In the Bible, he has revealed not only his law but also himself. We are encouraged to share our deepest thoughts and feelings through prayer and to meditate day and night on his Word.

The institution of the family was ordained by God from the beginning. When we examine how Genesis describes the nature of the pre-fall human relationship, we find an emphasis on intimacy, on the knowing of each other. We read in the Bible that Adam and Eve stood completely open and transparent before God. In their perfect humanity, Adam and Eve were naked before each other and felt no shame (Gen. 2:25). The intimacy they felt was the result of an ability to be themselves without pretense. They had no need to play deceptive games. Only after their disobedience did they try to hide from God out of a feeling of nakedness and shame. Shame is born out of the threat of being known intimately, and when fear is present, family members put on masks and begin to play deceptive roles with each other.

But when parent/child relationships are based on covenant and lived out in an atmosphere of grace and empowerment, we are more able to express ourselves honestly so we can know and be known by one another.

A concerted effort is made to listen, understand, and want what is best for the other. Differences are not only accepted, but uniqueness is valued and respected. This is how we are submissive and loving in relationships. We must be willing to give up something of our own needs and desires. When we come to our children with this kind of attitude and perspective, we will find a common ground of joy and satisfaction and mutual benefit.

The capacity for parents and children to freely communicate feelings with each other is contingent upon trust and commitment. We should not be afraid to share and be intimate with one another. John gives us insight into this in 1 John 4:16, 18, which reads: "God is love, and those who abide in love abide in God, and God abides in them. . . . There is no fear in love, but perfect love casts out fear; for fear has to do with punishment, and whoever fears has not reached perfection in love." God loves us perfectly, and we can respond out of that love, "We love because he first loved us" (1 John 4:19).

The earthly manifestation of unconditional love modeled in Jesus gives a picture of the type of communicative intimacy desirable in parent/child relationships. Recall how Jesus asked Peter not once but three times, "Do you love me?" at the end of his earthly ministry (John 21). Although there is no way of knowing the mind of Jesus during this encounter, it may be more than coincidental that Peter earlier had denied Jesus three times. Perhaps Jesus was giving Peter the opportunity to assert what he had previously denied. No doubt the relationship between Peter and Jesus had not been the same since Peter's triple betrayal. Likewise, family relationships become strained when we disappoint, fail, and even betray those whom we love the most.

Forgiving and being forgiven is an important part of renewal. It is a two-way street that can clear out the unfinished issues between family members, but in the process it puts us in a place of vulnerability. We must be willing to admit to our mistakes or admit to being offended. After all, the point of intimacy is that we need not be ashamed to admit failure and ask for forgiveness and reconciliation.

Conclusion

By examining biblical themes that have a bearing on the nature of parent/child relationships, we have suggested that:

- Children are the Lord's good gift, and the parent/child relationship is built on a unilateral covenant reflecting God's love. This unconditional love is given with the desire and hope that children will respond in love and commitment, just as God's children respond to him.

- The establishment and living out of parent/child relationships are to be done within an atmosphere of grace that embraces acceptance and forgiveness.
- Resources of parents and children are to be used to empower rather than to control one another.
- Intimacy is to be based on a knowing that leads to caring, understanding, communication, and communion with each other.

These four elements of Christian parent/child relationships are a continual process, whereby intimacy can lead to deeper covenant love, and commitment deepens through the grace freely offered. This acceptance and forgiveness allows for serving and empowering in relationships, and this sense of confidence leads to the ability to be intimate without fear, which in turn increases deep levels of communication and knowing.

This maturing of parent/child relationships enables family members to reach out to persons beyond the boundaries of the family. Living in covenant love is a dynamic process. God has designed family relationships to grow to maturity, which is analogous to the growth of individual believers "until all of us come to the unity of the faith and of the knowledge of the Son of God, to maturity, to the measure of the full stature of Christ" (Eph. 4:13).

Reflection Questions

1. Think of a time when you experienced the intimate "Abba, Father" connection. What were the circumstances that made this a profound moment for you? Tell a trusted friend or your spouse about this experience.

2. Read the prodigal son parable in Luke 15 and put yourself in the story. Which person(s) do you most identify with and why? Were there family members who showed you compassion and forgiveness when you were growing up? Think of ways in which God is a compassionate parent.

3. Take one of the four relationship principles (covenant, grace, empowerment, intimacy) and identify a specific event in your childhood when a parent or family member related to you in one of these ways. Share this with your spouse/friend or in a small group. Take time to give thanks for this person.

4. If you have not done so, complete part 2 of the Relationship-Empowerment Parenting Inventory in Appendix 1. There are a number of ways in which you can use the results to help understand yourself as a parent. You can begin by comparing your score for each of the four dimensions—commitment, grace, empowerment, and intimacy. Since we have found a fairly strong correlation between each of these dimensions, you might take note if your score on one is significantly lower than the others. For instance, if your score on the grace dimension is more than four points lower than the other dimensions, then it is worth your while to check your tendency to use shaming messages with your children. Then compare your scores with those of your spouse, using the results to discuss ways in which you relate to your children and ways in which you want to improve.

3

The Relationship-Empowerment Parenting Model

Empowerment Makes a Difference

Is there a person in your life who believes in you when you lack the confidence to believe in yourself? Do you have someone who helps you get beyond your self-imposed limitations? Did a parent, teacher, grandparent, relative, or friend equip you to develop your full potential as a child? If you answer "yes" to any of these questions, then you know what it is to be empowered. In fact, just thinking about the person who empowered you will undoubtedly bring a smile to your lips and a warm glow to your heart.

Take a moment right now to remember the special things this person(s) did to empower you. Perhaps it was a particular way they encouraged you; maybe it was how they stood by your side, cheering you on as you reached a long-awaited goal; or maybe it was the way they pointed out a potential in you that was hidden from your view. Regardless of how this person empowered you, because of him or her, your horizons were stretched and you became closer to whom God created you to be.

I hope you named a parent (or both parents) as an empowering person in your life. This is the highest compliment that can be given to a parent. In this chapter we will define empowerment, present a maturity-empowerment curve, provide practical suggestions about empowerment principles, and consider what it means to be empowered in Christ.

Empowering Components

- Assuring: "I'm on your side, and I believe in you."
- Encouraging: "You have strengths, gifts, and talents."
- Challenging: "I invite you to reach your potential."
- Equipping: "Here are basic truths and skills necessary to achieve success."
- Trusting: "I know you made a mistake, but I see you've learned from it."

What Is Empowerment?

A simple definition of power is the ability to influence. Of course, influence can be a negative or positive force. Power used to control others stymies growth, while power used for the good of others engenders growth. Empowerment requires active involvement and intentional engagement with our children. It involves building on our relationship and their natural talents to help them develop to their greatest potentials. It is the process of instilling confidence, teaching, guiding, equipping, challenging, strengthening, and building up children to become all they are meant to be.

Empowerment begins with the recognition that children are uniquely gifted by God to make a significant contribution in the world. Whether a child is able bodied or developmentally challenged, he or she has a purpose and meaning that can only be achieved by him or her. While affirming the specific strengths, talents, and gifts in each child, we should be careful to move with and not ahead of our children in terms of what we expect of them. In their own way and in their own time, they are able to meet expectations that are within their capacity and timetable.

The Relationship-Empowerment Model

In the Christian context, parents are committed to preparing their children to love God and their neighbors as themselves. Parenting for empowerment goes beyond developing personal strengths for "self" purposes. It offers the higher vision of serving others. Ultimately, we want our children to depend on God-ordained purposes for their validation.

The relationship-empowerment parenting model (REP) is similar to the New Testament concept of discipleship. Jesus established a vital relationship with his disciples. He challenged, nourished, equipped, taught, modeled, and empowered them to take over after the resurrection. He refused to use his power to control them and instead chose to serve them. He humbled himself when he washed their feet, he patiently explained when they couldn't make sense of his teaching, he was long-suffering with their unbelief and failures, and he never gave up hope but faithfully invested his life in them. He empowered them through an intentional, interpersonal relationship that connected them deeply with him and his purpose.

Empowerment always keeps the relationship in the forefront. Respect and encouragement are incentives to learn. Guard the relationship dynamics with all your heart. It's the secret to growing competent, self-determined children.

Mutual Empowerment

One of the great rewards of parenting is seeing our children become self-regulated and self-reliant. At this point, mutual empowerment is possible. I (Jack) remember well when my son Joel was able to give me tips on my tennis serve. I had taught him as a young boy, and he had gone on to perfect his skills through playing on high school and college tennis teams. He had become an excellent player and could offer suggestions to improve my game. This reciprocal giving and receiving in relationships is a good indication of relationship maturity. This is the ideal in our relationship with our children.

The Maturity-Empowerment Curve

Let's look at a visual representation of a maturity-empowerment curve. To begin with, there are two separate dimensions of parenting. One is parental affirmation, represented as low at the bottom and high at the top of the chart (see left side of chart). The other is parental guidance, represented as high at the left and low at the right (see bottom of chart). As true of the REP model, these two aspects of parenting are equally important and should not be thought of as separate entities.

An important contribution of the empowerment curve is that it helps us look at these two dimensions in terms of the maturity of the child. At the top of the chart, the maturity of the child is represented as low at the extreme left, moderate in the middle, and high at the extreme right. The parent/child dynamics adjust according to the age-appropriate ability. The "empowerment curve" indicates how different aspects of empowerment coincide with different levels of maturity and task achievement. You will note that at the extreme left end of the curve, children are quite

Figure 3.1

Maturity–Empowerment Curve

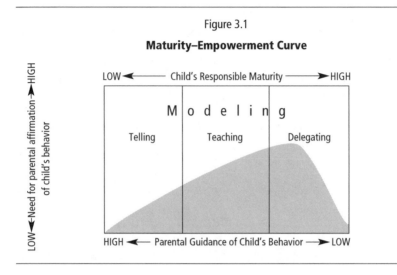

dependent on their parents, whereas at the extreme right there are high maturity and independence.

The four modalities of empowerment (modeling, telling, teaching, and delegating) are noted on the empowerment curve. While we continually use all four modalities throughout the empowerment parenting process, the particular task being learned will require being attuned to the maturity levels of the children. We must be flexible enough to adjust our focus and choose the modality that best fits with the changing needs of our children.

Modeling

Note how modeling transcends in an overarching way across the other modes of parenting on the empowerment curve. No doubt about it, modeling is the most effective tool for parents! When we practice what we preach, it's living proof that our beliefs and actions harmonize. We say what we do and we do what we say, and that congruent, consistent living gives credibility to who we are and what we teach.

Modeling is a constant in the lives of our children no matter what their level of maturity. Even when our kids take on more responsibility for themselves, they still need support for any new task. Take the example of your son becoming a baby-sitter. On-the-job training is the best way to learn and gain confidence. So you go along to participate with him (modeling modality) and show him the ropes. You give him hints and moral support as he cares for the baby. Initially, you may demonstrate how to soothe the baby by using a variety of calming techniques. He observes how you hold the baby, rock, sing a song, give a bottle, go for a walk with the stroller, etc. While you give some instruction, he learns best by watching. Then you step back as he takes over the next time the baby cries. You coach, encourage, and affirm him as he learns the role. You acknowledge his resourcefulness when he comes up with a creative idea such as swinging the baby back and forth in the baby seat. Through participating, he learns the task and gradually becomes confident. Then he is ready to be on his own, because he has become a competent baby-sitter.

Telling

It's not long after our children are born that we begin using the telling mode. We say, "Don't touch the stove, it's hot!" We explain, "Brushing our teeth keeps them clean." In a myriad of ways, we give them knowledge that empowers. (The telling mode is especially useful when children are young and unable to do things on their own.)

This parenting modality is characterized by one-way communication. Parents simply tell their children what, where, when, and how to do things in the beginning, without much need for affirmation. However, when children begin to take on a task, affirmation must be high to encourage them in the learning process. For example, when your child first learns to tie her shoes, you tell her exactly what to do and how to do it. She watches carefully but must get her own fingers working around the loop to make it happen.

The telling and teaching are high at the beginning, but support and affirmation become extremely important during the delegation stage. It is very difficult when first learning a task, and strong encouragement keeps the child from being discouraged. So we praise him as he tries and tries and tries again. He may get frustrated, but since we believe in him and let him know he is improving, he will most likely keep at it until he finally masters it on his own. Once the task becomes part of his life, he no longer needs to be affirmed for doing it. The internal reinforcement of the accomplishment is sufficient reward. It would be odd to praise him for something he's already conquered. He's now on to bigger and better things and needs our support for the new tasks he's attempting at the moment.

Teaching

The teaching modality differs from telling because communication is now two-way. When you visit the zoo, you're likely to observe parents participating in the fine art of teaching their children, reading information off the exhibit placards, and answering their curious questions. Early childhood is that wonderful time when natural curiosity opens up a wealth of information about the world, when kids seem to have an endless capacity to take in an enormous amount of teaching.

The teaching modality is especially helpful when children are taking on more responsibility for functions of self-care. They need specific instruction and information to do the task well, and engaging them through dialogue and answering questions provides the needed empowerment. For example, when your daughter takes on the family laundry as her chore, you spend time telling and teaching her the hows and whys of sorting clothes, you give instruction about the amount of detergent to add to the clothes, what fabric selections to use, etc. You answer her questions to clarify and provide reasons why you don't mix dark colors with white. Then as she takes on the task, you praise her for doing her chore well, like "You fold the clothes so neatly!" Mistakes are bound to occur—the clothes might come out of the washing machine with a pink glow because a red sweatshirt was added to the whites. This too becomes an important part of the learning, and she makes corrections accordingly. Once she is proficient, she no longer needs continued instruction or affirmation. Of course, compliments from family members about how nice it is to have clean clothes laid out on their beds each week are always welcome.

Teaching as empowerment can be an exciting and rewarding interaction between us and our children, especially if it's experienced as a time of enjoyment. However, if we are obsessed with pouring information into our children for the sake of impressing others, learning takes on a coercive bent. High-pressure perfectionism and daunting expectations are clearly barriers to learning and disruptive of the parent/child relationship.

I (Judy) have a regretful memory of teaching my nine-year-old daughter how to play the piano. My powerful presence standing over her while she practiced "until she got it right" was an exasperating experience for both of us. Being overly invested in her achievement at the piano because of my own musical background, I failed to recognize her discomfort and disinterest. I didn't allow her to discover the joy of music in her own way.

Delegating

Wise parents delegate! In the later stages of parenting, we naturally do less talking and more delegating. As children approach preteen and teenage years, they make choices and are responsible for their actions. By the time they reach this stage, we are no longer telling them what to do, because they are now doing it for themselves. Now our task is to let go.

Teaching a child how to drive a car is a good example of the delegating modality. When my (Jack's) dad decided it was time for me to learn how to drive the car, I was excited but also a little nervous. My father, a rather shy Norwegian man, was known for his walk and not his talk. I wondered how my dad would give me the proper instruction I needed to pass my driver's test. I thought maybe it would be better to go to driver's training. Yet I had observed my dad driving for years and knew he had an excellent driving record. So we proceeded.

On my first day behind the wheel, the car sputtered, jerked, and leaped forward when I was learning to shift. Through it all, my dad remained calm, gave simple directions to correct my movements, and showed confidence in my abilities. One day while we were practicing backing up, I ran into a small tree. Shaking with fear, I said I was sorry and jumped out of the driver's seat. Dad checked the back fender and then told me to get back in the driver's seat. "When I got bucked off the horse in South Dakota, my father told me to get right back on!" Dad said. The message was clear: One can learn from a mistake and do it right the next time.

What goes around comes around! When my son Joel was learning to drive, I went through a similar scenario. I was better at giving instructions, so there weren't as many trial-and-error mistakes. But one day while driving in the mountains, I found a good place to practice backing up. Unfortunately, Joel backed into a huge Sequoia tree. "Joel, couldn't you see that tree?" was my first response. Then I remembered those wise words of my father. So we checked out the bumper, and I repeated the message of my dad and grandpa before me: "Get back in the driver's seat, son. I know you can do it this time."

All the proper instruction we could possibly give about driving is not enough. And all they've learned by observing our driving is not enough. Now we must be willing to delegate and trust our teenagers to do the driving without us.

Letting Go Is the Hardest Part

The difficult thing about the delegating modality is letting go. Sometimes we may need to give our children a gentle nudge so they can spread their wings and learn to fly. If we fail to give our blessing for the flight, they may never dare leave the nest. While spreading their wings may be a fearful idea, and they may falter during their first solo flight, unless they take that risk they'll never be empowered to soar. So like the mother eagle who pushes her babies over the edge of the nest but glides beneath to catch them when they falter, empowering parents delegate responsibility, step back, and allow their children to make their decisions on their own. We will be there to lend a supporting hand if they falter, but only after they've taken flight.

We (the Pipers) were challenged when our daughter Karlie decided to take a semester off college and go to Africa to work in a mission. This was an expensive dream and a scary one for us. But Karlie was determined to raise as much money as she needed to get there. She discussed her plans with us and asked for our input on how to plan for the trip. Together we figured the cost of travel, personal expenses, passports, and health-care preparation. We brainstormed for possible sources of income, and Karlie worked long hours at her summer job.

When we came up with an idea, we turned it over to Karlie. She took charge and made the decision whether or not to follow through on the idea. It was her adventure, her dream, and her job to earn money to get there. Through a variety of ways, she reached her financial goal, took care of an enormous number of details, and found herself on her way to Africa.

Let children make mistakes? You've got to be kidding! How can we stand back and watch them move toward disaster? Our instinct is to protect them, because we're acutely aware of the grave consequences of even one mistake. However, if they are frozen by an inability to make choices, this is another kind of tragedy. Hopefully, life teaches us from the mistakes we make so we won't repeat them. And certainly we can help our children think through their choices by asking good questions, acknowledging the fearfulness, and believing they have what it takes to meet their personal challenges. In order to help them reach their potential, we need to stretch beyond our own fears that they can't make it without us. We empower our children to meet the risky ventures of life by letting them fly, not by refusing to let them try.

A Lesson in Empowerment

Some parents have the false impression that as children grow older and become more powerful, parents lose power. This notion is completely contrary to empowerment as a principle. We as parents remain powerful and influential. We do not yield to the whims of our children but instead support and guide them toward responsible interdependence. We use our rightful leadership to prepare our children to live as healthy, mature adults, capable of building and maintaining a strong network of meaningful relationships. All along, we keep the relationship at the heart of our parenting approach. Notice how the following story illustrates empowerment in the context of the relationship.

In Tom's life, a number of empowerment components came together. Tom was asked by his teacher to give a speech during the high school assembly. He was thrilled that the teacher thought enough of him to ask, but he was also bombarded with self-doubts about whether he could pull off the task. When he got home that night, he talked to his father, Jerry, about it. Jerry listened carefully as his son spoke with excitement about the idea but also hinted at his fears about the challenge. Jerry congratulated his son on the honor but also acknowledged his feelings of inadequacy. He gave his support by promising to read over Tom's first draft and give him honest feedback. This response conveyed his belief in his son's ability to write a speech, as well as provided active support that would help Tom achieve his goal.

A few days later, Tom rather nervously handed the rough draft to Jerry but was calmed when Jerry carefully pointed out the strengths, asked questions that stimulated additional ideas, and gave some helpful suggestions about the phrasing of some sentences. Tom appreciated the positive and insightful interaction with his dad. He was relieved that there had not been one degrading negative criticism! Instead, his father equipped him through kind and concrete ideas that renewed his confidence to do a rewrite.

When Tom wanted to practice his speech, he asked his dad to listen to him. And Jerry not only listened with respect but also offered a few pointers about Tom's delivery. Then he expressed his congratulations on a job well done with a high-five gesture.

When Tom gave his speech the next day, he did so with self-satisfaction and confidence. When the applause came at the end of his speech, Tom was thrilled with the response. His work and effort had paid off, building up his confidence. He took the credit for what he had done, but he also learned how important it was to have the support of significant people in his life. His teacher had given him an opportunity to develop his talent, and his father had empowered him to succeed.

Empowered by God

Empowerment is a biblical principle. Being created in the image of God, our children have the potential to become what God intends them to be. In fact, they have the capacity to go beyond human limitations, as the Holy Spirit empowers them to live extraordinary and abundant lives in Christ's strength. We can encourage their growth in Christ by noticing changes, pointing out progress, and showing awareness of personal sacrifices. Empowerment occurs when we challenge faulty thinking and actions, point out consequences of behavior, and help our teens follow and keep God's directives. Learning to depend on God is what we want to model to our children.

Depending on God as a source of maturity means being empowered in Christ. Becoming obedient to God's way is the true path to maturity, because it is God's Spirit that prompts the heart and provides the capacity to forgive, stand up for righteous causes, and speak out boldly for one's convictions. Choosing God's way rather than somebody else's way is the key to fulfillment.

When our children have identities that are firmly planted in Christ, they can grasp the deeper spiritual meaning of who they are. It is Jesus who ultimately changes our lives, heals our wounds, draws us to himself, and empowers us to follow a godly path. While human relationships within the family challenge and shape us, it is God who convicts and gives us the spiritual power to change.

When as parents we stand in solidarity with Christ's way and look to the Holy Spirit to empower us, we show our humble dependence on God. The hope for us and our children is Christ at the center, being rooted, built up and established in the faith. In Christ, we are to show "compassion, kindness, humility, meekness, and patience" (Col. 3:12). The family provides a place where members can celebrate a common meaning and purpose that goes beyond themselves. Anchored in Christ, the family works, lives, worships, and has their being in Christ Jesus.

Reflection Questions

1. List all the ways empowering takes place in your home. Decide what you can do to increase mutual empowerment between family members.
2. Make an effort this week to do one or two empowering acts each day. Make note of the difference it makes. Determine to make a habit of it!
3. See Part 3 of appendix 1 (p. 197) for an exercise that will assist you in assessing your strengths and limitations on the maturity-empowerment curve.

4

Dimensions of Parenting
That Empower

"So what do we do with the research information and biblical principles offered in the first three chapters of this section?" you might ask. Since we've told you not to wait with bated breath for the next "gem" of wisdom uttered by the next how-to-do-it prophets of child rearing, you may wonder if we're going to leave you bone dry, without offering any practical pointers. This is a good challenge for us! While we *do* want you to listen to your inner sensibility about forming a unique relationship with each of your children and your personal wisdom about empowering them to reach their potential, we also want to share practical suggestions with you. In fact, when we surveyed parents about what they would find helpful in a parenting book, every one of them wanted the specific nuts and bolts behind the theory.

So with this in mind, we will introduce some important dimensions of the REP model in this chapter and get age and stage specific in the next section. In chapters 5 through 10 of part 2, we will address developmental considerations, relationship principles, specific behavioral issues, and concrete ideas on discipline that empowers. Then, knowing how hard parents are on themselves, we will end each chapter with a section entitled "Parents Are Human Too!" Aware of the tremendous responsibility it is to be an effective parent, we humbly admit that we need all the help we can to do our job well.

The REP model offers a dynamic view of parent/child interaction and interdependency. When there is a correct balance of being responsible as a parent and taking on responsibility as a child, maximum development is possible. Parents may ask themselves the question, "Do my interactions and discipline facilitate or hinder responsible maturity in my child?" while children may ask themselves, "Am I capable of doing this myself, or am I not taking sufficient responsibility?" It is discovering the "right amount" on both sides that brings out the best in us, just as the right amount of seasoning brings out the best flavors in a gourmet meal. Either too much or too little can ruin the stew, so to speak.

With this in mind, we offer three dimensions of parenting that empower parents and children to achieve reciprocal responsibility. The first dimension is the concept of scaffolding, whereby parents support a child in any particular task just beyond their present capability. The second dimension is building the relationship, where there is a flow of give-and-take in interaction and communication. The third dimension is empowering children through the use of natural and logical consequences toward responsible behavior and social interaction. We'll also provide practical insight about how to bring these dimensions to bear on parenting that empowers.

Scaffolding Dimension

The REP model promotes empowerment as the most essential way to develop secure, competent children who cultivate a self in relation to God and others. But how does a parent learn what's the proper amount of support? Is there a range within which a child cannot quite accomplish a task without help? On the other hand, how much help is too much? The scaffold metaphor can provide some insight into these questions.

While touring Hong Kong, we (Jack and Judy) were amazed at the bamboo scaffolding surrounding the huge skyscrapers. We couldn't imagine how the scaffolding could provide the proper support, because it looked so flimsy. But as we later learned, it was the flexibility in the scaffolding that was so useful to building those strong, tall buildings. The bamboo poles formed an outer structure that allowed the workers to do what needed to be done, after which the scaffolding was removed.

We as parents provide a similar temporary support structure while our children are growing up. We must be able to extend a bit, but not too much beyond the child's capacity, so they can be confident in learning and developing their abilities. Our scaffold needs to be flexible in response to our children's continuing development. And we must be willing to remove the scaffold when it's no longer needed.

What makes this so tricky is that normal oscillation occurs every time our children learn new tasks. We cannot take away the structure too soon, because the cement is still drying. For example, learning to walk is accomplished in gradual increments. When a child takes his first steps,

Tips for Scaffolding

- Know what's age appropriate
- Be in tune with your child's unique way
- Pay attention to your child's style of learning
- Give enough but not too much support
- Allow mistakes to become avenues of change

he is cautious, teeters, catches his balance, and falls down more than he walks. He can go faster by crawling (no need for scaffolding), but he's encouraged to take steps while grasping fingers for support (more scaffolding). Coaxing and praise by parents becomes an incentive to take the courageous next step, but if pushed too hard, the child may refuse and plop himself down. He may even resort to taking steps when his parents aren't looking. On the other hand, if parents don't give enough encouragement, he may delay learning to walk and be content to sit or crawl.

Remember, children have tremendous curiosity and eagerness to explore their world, so our job is to be "in tune" with their timing. A new challenge pops up once an old one is conquered. After walking, there is the thrill of learning to run, jump, skip, etc. This is the natural way children learn to master tasks throughout their lives. But unique differences keep us on our toes. Since some children crawl on their tummies instead of their knees and some go backward instead of forward, parents must make a scaffold that fits the particular needs of each particular child.

Relationship Dimension

Our premise is that God created human beings to develop in and through intimate relationship. Therefore, it's natural that we feel so strongly about the parent/child relationship. When we hold that precious bundle in our arms, we feel awe and wonderment, knowing that our lives are changed forever. Through this personal relationship, our interactions, behaviors, and connections shape us. We become new people through the parenting journey.

Because God has made us, there is something of God's image within us, urging us to become the people God wants us to be. Often God uses the relationships we have with our children to help us make changes and to become more like Christ. Paul writes in Corinthians that "all of us, with unveiled faces, seeing the glory of the Lord as though reflected in a mirror, are being transformed into the same image from one degree of glory to another; for this comes from the Lord, the Spirit" (2 Cor. 3:18). In other words, we are in the process of being molded into the image of Christ through the work of the Holy Spirit as we parent. So the developing relationship is not only important for our children but for our growth as well. Yet feeling the strength and safety of the parent/child relationship will be a foundation for mature development in children.

The REP model is based on our belief that a secure attachment provides a safe haven in which relationships can develop. And being sufficiently connected gives people a capacity to be socially responsible and interdependent. Having a healthy self is needed in order to engage in and establish mature interdependence with others. Paradoxically, the more one is aware of the self, the greater is one's capacity for making significant connections with others.

The relational dimension of parenting involves viewing misbehavior from our children's perspective. If we can put ourselves in our children's shoes and look at behavior from their viewpoint, we'll better understand how to exercise discipline. In fact, misbehavior quite often is the result of children's "mistaken" ideas of what's happening around them. Here are some typical mistaken ideas of children and how parents can respond (Dreikurs, 1958):

Child's Mistaken Goals	Parents' Effective Response
Child wants attention	Give attention when not demanded
Child wants power	Remove self from power struggle
Child wants revenge	Avoid retaliation/win child over
Child wants encouragement	Affirm/encourage child

Attention Seeking

When a child constantly is seeking attention, we usually feel annoyed and exasperated. It seems as if the child can never get enough of our time. And if we reprimand or pull away, the child often acts out with more disturbing behavior, which inadvertently gets even more attention.

A more effective response is to ignore the child when she demands attention, but give her special attention when she's *not* asking for it. Your ability to understand her mistaken goal—"I only count when I'm the center of attention"—signals an important message. The child needs attention. However, you don't want to reinforce her insistence for it during inappropriate times.

For example, say you have friends over for coffee, and she is constantly interrupting and whining for your attention. If you continually give in to her, you'll no doubt be angry and embarrassed in front of your friends. So after you've told her nicely that you don't want to be interrupted, ignore her if she keeps it up. You may try to divert her with other activities but then be clear that you won't respond to her interruptions. Now here's the key point! Since you understand that she has a need for extra attention from you, you should now look for opportunities to give it to her. Find unsuspecting times and then give her your full attention. For example, when she's playing quietly with her dolls, go over and play with her. Let her know you enjoy being with her and do it frequently. If you satisfy her deeper need, she will no longer need to disrupt you. You will have been able to meet her need without reinforcing the demand for it.

Power Struggle

When a child says no and refuses your requests, you are most likely in a power struggle. It's the child's mistaken idea that he only counts when he has his way. And you most likely feel angry back and want to show him you're the boss! This common battle usually intensifies into a no-win standoff that leads to angry emotional outbursts. You may be big enough to overpower him, but he can wail and carry on to let you know he's not given up.

The better strategy is for you to remove yourself from the power struggle. Since you are the mature adult, you can decide to stay out of such a battle. By merely removing yourself from the emotional struggle, you can calmly go about your business without getting caught up in a fight. It's empowering to walk away with dignity, refusing to lower yourself to his level.

Once again, though, the key is to put yourself in his shoes and try to understand why he needs to feel more powerful. You may ask yourself if there's something frustrating him, if he's feeling a lack of competence with his friends at school or in his life, etc. This is an opportunity to check things out at a deeper level. Are you still controlling things he can do for himself? Are you being patient when he tries to do things for himself, or do you hurry him along? Do you let him take responsibility? This is an opportunity for you to ask relationship questions to find out why the power struggles are occurring. Talk to him about it so you can change what needs changing.

Revenge

We're told in Scripture not to provoke our children to anger. But sometimes we push them too hard and damage the relationship so badly that they are unforgiving and close their hearts toward us. A child who wants to get back at you is expressing deep, negative feelings about the relationship. She is hurt and wants to get even. You as a parent may feel hurt and mad too, and you may even want to get back at her.

But the important thing is not to retaliate with a similar vengeful attitude. As the adult, you are wise enough to look for the deeper dynamics behind inappropriate behaviors. When you see things from her perspective, you'll often recognize the seriousness of her hurt, and you'll want to soften your approach and try to win her back. No offense is worth risking the relationship.

Here you need to draw on God's strength and go the second or third mile necessary for reconciliation. Extricate yourself from her hurtful actions, maintain order with restraint, and take the time to listen with compassion and understanding. A family therapist may help to get to the bottom of the pain. Or sometimes setting a time apart in a family gathering for mutual confession, forgiveness, and reconciliation can provide the healing that's necessary.

Encouragement

When a child gives up, it is probably the most gut-wrenching experience for parents. You may despair and feel hopeless yourself, not knowing what to do or how to help your child. You may not have a clue about what has put him in such a funk, and efforts to encourage him seem to be wasted.

Finding a way to enter into his world is the key response. You must try to understand what's happening to him. A youth leader, pastor, or teacher may be the one who can safely unravel his feelings of inadequacy. It is important not to feel threatened when your child talks to or gets help from another trusted adult. Sometimes, he may be able to express himself through art or other creative means. In severe cases, a therapist may be needed to help him out of his discouraged state of mind. Hang in there! He needs you now more than ever. If *you* give up, things will only get worse. You may need a place of support for yourself.

The following story shows how a sensitive father empowered a discouraged son. Even though this was not a serious situation, it illustrates what happens when a parent sees things from a child's point of view and is able to be present in the pain.

Nine-year-old Colin was having a difficult time with a few classmates. He felt left out and sad. His father, Jim, tried to encourage Colin by reminding him that he was a great student and had lots of friends, and that maybe he was making too much of this situation, but that didn't help. From Colin's perspective, his world was coming apart, and his fears were real.

So Jim took time to listen and allow Colin to express his hurt feelings. This empathy allowed Colin to acknowledge the sad feelings rather than be talked out of them. Then Jim suggested that his son take time to draw pictures or write down his feelings about what was happening. When Colin shared the pictures, Jim recognized the bullying his son was facing from two or three boys in particular. The meanness and negative impact was real. So Jim gathered his family together, and they made a list of adjectives to describe Colin's positive qualities. This way he felt his family's support.

After taking the time to listen, Jim was reminded of a similar childhood experience he'd had. He told Colin about a time in his life when he too felt isolated. This father/son sharing opened up a new level of connection. Colin could see that his father also had a desire to be liked and that he knew how it felt to be rejected.

These events happened over a period of several weeks. During that time, Jim and his wife talked to Colin's teacher about the situation so she could be alert to what was happening. In addition, Jim suggested that Colin write a story about this experience. Colin really got into it and did a PowerPoint presentation of the whole event. He included a section about how God knew his heart and his sadness and courage. Jim wondered if Colin would like to bring the PowerPoint presentation to Sunday school class (a place where he felt affirmed and accepted) to share with other kids who might be going through a similar problem. This further empowered Colin, as the presentation turned into a helpful discussion for the other kids. In fact, Jim and Colin allowed us to share their story in our book as a way of helping parents and their children who are discouraged. A painful experience, when handled with care, can bring a deeper understanding that has an empowering ending.

Discipline Dimension

The root word of discipline means "to learn." While parenting is a mutual learning experience, parents are called to take the leadership position. It is our responsibility to teach, guide, direct, correct, model, and discipline our children. Strong parents are confident, effective, powerful, and genuine in their ability to discipline. They communicate reasons for what they ask for and help their children develop internal control and social agency.

We'd like to take a moment to make a distinction between discipline and punishment. The primary goal of discipline is to stay connected relationally while correcting and disciplining for future maturity and empowerment. In contrast, punishment is often an arbitrary action that does not take the relationship dynamics into account.

Discipline and Punishment Differences

Discipline:	Punishment:
Trains for correction and maturity	Inflicts penalty
Focuses on future change	Focuses on past misdeeds
Is done out of love and concern	Shows emotional reactivity of the parents
Eliminates power struggles	Initiates power struggles
Offers security to the child	Instills fear and guilt in child
Enhances internal responsibility	Focuses on external behavior and obedience

There are a number of discipline approaches designed to change a child's behavior. We will comment briefly on the first four approaches, which use external means to control behavior but do little to inculcate internal responsibility. We'll then focus on natural and logical consequences, which put the focus on internal responsibility and social interest.

External Control

Reinforcement

Reinforcement is rewarding positive actions so they are more likely to be repeated. An example is giving M&Ms to reinforce potty-training success. But while the candy becomes an incentive, a child may focus more on the external treat rather than the internal pride of learning bodily control. Praise also reinforces behaviors but can inadvertently become an external reward as well.

Extinction

Extinction is another behavioral approach that works. Basically, it is *not* reinforcing negative behavior with attention, so that the behavior will be eliminated. When parents ignore troublesome habits, for example, the behavior usually stops. Of course, there are misbehaviors that cannot be ignored, so this is a limited solution.

Spanking

Spanking is the use of physical means to stop a behavior. Many parents are opposed to corporal punishment, but those parents who do use this modality generally find it to be effective. Our main criticism is that spanking uses an external rather than an internal locus of control. A child will relinquish the negative behavior out of a desire to stay out of trouble, not for any internally motivated reason. In the absence of the parent, however, "anything goes" because internal control hasn't been instilled. In addition, spanking can cause a serious breach in the parent/child relationship, because most parents administer physical punishment with negative emotions. Anger, harsh words, and out-of-control behavior can elicit feelings of hate, resentment, defeat, or insecurity in the heart of the child. For these reasons, we don't recommend spanking as a mode of discipline. We believe there are more creative ways to deal with misbehavior that keeps the focus on internal control and the relationship intact.

Love Withdrawal

Love withdrawal is not only a negative method of discipline, but it is contrary to the biblical concept of covenant love. When parental love is withdrawn, children become desperate and will do almost anything to stay connected. So while it is a powerful way to control behavior, it's at the expense of the child. Love withdrawal triggers deep fears of rejection in children, and obedience out of fear turns children into people pleasers who do not learn to think and act responsibly. It's an external approach that damages internal self-concept and makes children feel they are not worthy or loveable.

Internal Responsibility

Rudolf Dreikurs and Vickie Scholtz in *Children: The Challenge* (1964) and Don Dinkmeyer and Gary McKay (1976), founders of STEP (Systematic Training for Effective Parenting), espouse natural and logical consequences as the best way to raise responsible children. These educators offer practical and widely accepted ways to discipline children, emphasizing a method that empowers children to be internally disciplined and relationally minded. These ideas correspond nicely with the REP model.

In contrast to the other approaches, children learn internal control and responsibility through facing the consequences of their behaviors. They then can see that their actions and choices impact other people in a positive or negative way. The goal is to cooperate with others rather than to behave out of self-interest alone, bringing about regard for self and others.

Logical Consequences

Logical consequences are fair and reasonable rules that help children learn limits and become responsible for their behavior. For example, before Bobby is old enough to know that passing cars can be dangerous, he is told he must not go in the street. He must stay in the yard when he plays, or else he will have to come inside. The consequence for overstepping the limit is clearly understood—"If you open the gate, you will come inside and won't be able to play in the yard for a while." Bobby's parents must be vigilant and watch for him to test the limits. When he does, they must immediately take him inside.

The point is for the parents to make no exceptions, even when the child protests. If Bobby cries or is angry about the consequence, his parents must carry through in a firm, calm manner. They must let Bobby know that he has overstepped the limit and therefore must come in the house for a certain amount of time. Time inside will give Bobby time to think about what he did and help him understand that consequences will be carried out. Be sure that the consequence (time inside) is appropriate for the child's age.

There is no need for a verbal reprimand or put-down—"Didn't I tell you that was dangerous! You are a bad boy, and now you must come inside." Such an emotional reprimand will focus Bobby's feelings on himself for being bad, rather than focusing on his internal responsibility to stay in the yard.

Principles of Logical Consequence	Child's Likely Response
Puts emphasis on social interaction and relationship	Feels self-respect and respect for others
Logically relates consequences to the misbehavior	Gains self-discipline
Separates the deed from the doer	Feels acceptable even if behavior is unacceptable
Presents choice	Learns from experience
Communicates respect and goodwill	Develops a cooperative spirit
Is oriented toward change	Becomes self-directing

Natural Consequences

Natural consequences are the unavoidable responses that occur naturally as a result of a certain behavior, whether or not an adult is present. Take the example of five-year-old June rocking back and forth in a rocking chair. The rocking brings her pleasure and joy, but if she becomes too rambunctious, the chair will fall over. In other words, she suffers the consequences of rocking too rigorously. This negative experience helps her monitor her behavior the next time she rocks in the chair. Children find their limits in these natural ways. Mistakes help them set parameters for future actions.

Parents can take advantage of this natural phenomenon by simply staying out of the way and allowing children to learn from their experiences. A child who throws sand is bound to get some in her eyes; the teenager who doesn't do his homework will be given a detention. This is how things work in the real world.

There are times, of course, when natural consequences put a child in danger. We can't allow a child to run into the street, because the natural consequence is being hit by a passing car. So in this case we need to move to logical consequences as a corrective.

Practical Steps on How to Set Up and Carry Out Consequences

Consequences are thoughtful and deliberate plans designed to develop intrinsic motivation. When planning a consequence, we must make sure that the consequence is directly related to the misbehavior, so it will make sense to the child. Once the consequence is well defined, it will be easy for us to follow through in a matter-of-fact way—we won't have to think on our feet or try to devise a punishment in the heat of the moment. Since it's already understood that certain misbehaviors will lead to certain consequences, we can take swift action while remaining calm and loving.

If we inappropriately set up consequences of behavior, however, we defeat the purpose. Consequences should be clear and related to the misbehavior, but if they are too severe, they will backfire. If a consequence is given with an attitude ("I'll show you! You deserve what you're getting!") or is set up out of revenge ("I'll get you to shape up this time!"), then we have entered into an emotional power struggle. Under these circumstances, our children are provoked to anger or revenge rather than being challenged to change behavior.

Consequences delivered in an unreasonable, coercive manner will fail as well. When a child hits the dog, we should make her stay inside the house for a reasonable amount of time, not all day. She needs enough time to think about what she did and hopefully feel sorry for her mistake. (By the way, make sure she isn't doing something she's observed other family members doing.) And when she resumes play, comment when she is nice to the dog, which reinforces positive behavior.

Common Pitfalls of Parents

Feeling sorry for the child and giving in to protests
Taking a punitive attitude with emotional reactivity
Being inconsistent
Failing to follow through in a firm, matter-of-fact way
Talking too much (act, don't talk)
Rubbing it in—getting pleasure out of humiliating the child

Using natural and logical consequences respects the dignity of the child *and* the parent, enhancing the relationship connection. When enforcing a consequence, we may express mild regret, i.e., "I'm sorry you have to come in for hitting the dog. I'm sure when you think about how much it hurt him, you'll be able to ask me to put him in the garage the next time he bothers you." By communicating in this way, we show confidence in our children. We communicate options, so the kids have a different way of handling things the next time.

Another helpful tip is to evaluate how we handled a certain situation. Ask yourself questions like, How did I act? What were my words? What emotions came up for me and how did I contain them? Was the consequence given with kindness as well as firmness? Did it serve the purpose? For example, if a child has a lot of toys, it doesn't make a difference to take one away for a week. In this case, we must ask if the purpose was accomplished. If not, we should decide on a better consequence for the next time. Evaluating what we've done will help us become increasingly consistent and more creative in devising effective consequences.

One final thing to keep in mind is that there is a learning curve when it comes to setting consequences. We may be quite appalled at the anger we feel when disciplining children. We won't always do this perfectly. Sometimes we'll lose our tempers and carry out consequences in a negative way. But after we evaluate our reactions, we should talk it over with our children. There is no shame in admitting when we blew it. But the good news is that regular use of logical consequences gives a great deal of confidence as we learn to contain our reactive responses and simply follow through with consistency and firmness.

Discipline is a huge task for parents. It not only includes correcting and changing behavior but also communicating values and teaching problem-solving and relationship skills. But the promise of Scripture is that good training pays off. The end result is that our children become internally motivated, self-disciplined, and focused on others.

Make Use of Family Meetings As a Time to Talk and Empower

Routine family meetings can give children a perfect opportunity to participate in family life. The meeting should be in a comfortable atmosphere where the members can discuss what's happening in the family. Each member's ideas and feelings should be welcomed and honored, and suggestions must be taken seriously. Even the youngest child should be included. Topics can range from family chores, vacations, struggles between siblings, consequences for behaviors, goals, planning fun events, etc.

The family meeting is a practical way of modeling the cooperative nature of family life. It teaches tolerance and respect in relationships, and it is a good place to air relationship struggles and talk about the normal hurts and conflicts between family members. It can be a place where reconciliation, forgiveness, and restoration can occur.

The parents should take leadership, ensuring democratic principles of fairness and free expression. When children are old enough, they may take turns chairing the meeting, which teaches them leadership skills. The chair starts the meeting, sets the agenda, appoints a recorder, and closes the meeting on time. The agenda is set by the family members, whether it is to negotiate a rule, address a change in the family schedule, suggest a fun activity, or request a change in chores. The chair keeps an eye on the clock so the agenda can be managed in the time set aside. The chair also makes sure that everyone has a chance to give input and that family members speak in an orderly fashion. Topics are dealt with one at a time until there is agreement on a solution or a decision to "table" the discussion for the next meeting.

Family rules, discipline, and consequences are determined through discussion, dialogue, and negotiation. Every member is very much a part of the decision-making process. Although parents should determine consequences for young children, there is a time when children are able to take part in setting up consequences for misbehaviors. And consequences should be developed for all family members as an equitable arrangement! If the family rule is "no dishes should be left in the sink after supper," then every family member must submit to the consequence. Therefore, if Dad "forgets," he must clean up the dishes the next morning and empty the dishwasher like any other family member.

Here's an example from our (the Balswick) family, who had a dilemma about using the common bathroom shower. It became a negative scene, especially for Judy, whenever someone failed to clean hair out of the drain. So we met together to brainstorm ideas about a consequence for this behavior. Here were some brainstorming ideas: the offender could not shower for a week, the offender would need to scrub down the shower the next day, the offender should write a note of apology to the family, the offender would have to use the basement shower for a week, etc. You get the point! All ideas were taken down and then discussed. Our family finally decided that the offender would scrub the shower the next day. And the rule applied to everyone, Mom and Dad included. Wow, did we have a well-scrubbed shower for the next few weeks! But you know what? Soon there was no hair left in the drain. This consequence taught regard for others in sharing common space and the importance of considering how others are impacted by your actions.

The family meeting is also a time to report on positive things happening in each person's life and to plan family events. It is a time when family members listen to each other and create cooperative ways for the family to meet the needs of each member as well as consider the family as a unit.

Parents Are Human Too!

It's tough being a parent! The truth is, it's hard getting up in the middle of the night with infants, and it's difficult living with a teenager. (It's a shock when your child progresses from talking to talking back!) And sometimes, even more difficult, we often have to face things about ourselves and become profoundly aware of our limitations, failures, and vulnerabilities. And one area where we may be vulnerable is our marriages. We as authors caution you that children can impact a marriage for better or worse. Having children can weaken this bond unless we take proper care to protect our spousal relationships.

Spouses are human as well! We rub each other the wrong way as we work out the parenting role. Strong emotions (anger, hurt, disappointment) raise their ugly heads more easily than we ever thought they would. Of course, all couples have disagreements. That's not the issue. It's how we deal with conflict that matters. When we soften our words, give compassionate responses, listen with empathy, soothe ourselves in order to de-escalate emotional reactivity, and stay emotionally connected even during a fight, this makes all the difference.

The quality of the marriage is the most important resource for effective parenting. We need to stay emotionally connected throughout the parenting stages. Here are some practical hints for keeping marriages strong.

- Protect the sacred "Us" of the relationship
- Be committed, reliable, and responsible

- Make every effort to please your spouse
- Humbly accept differences—your way is not the only way
- Maintain fairness in parenting and housework
- Do unto your spouse what they want you to do
- Invest in your spouse so they feel valued
- Stay best friends
- Take quality time to be/pray together
- Focus on the positive aspects of your marriage

Happy couples do hundreds of things for each other every day, so be active in this area. Keep your sense of humor. Learn to lighten up and not take yourself too seriously. Make a practice of forgiving yourself as well as other family members. Create a gracing atmosphere. Guard your spousal relationship with all your efforts. You've heard it said before, but it's worth repeating—the best thing you can do for your children is to be a good and loving spouse.

Staying close and connected helps us deal effectively with differences, share our deeper feelings, dreams, and desires with each other, and work toward a united purpose in parenting. Continually count your blessings and thank God for your spouse and your children.

Thank goodness God isn't through with us yet! Most of us find parenting to be the most challenging thing we've ever done, but we can be hopeful that the Holy Spirit continues to work change in us. While we physically grow our children up, they grow us up emotionally. And in the process, God is changing us too!

Reflection Questions

1. In regard to the scaffolding dimension, give an example of being overprotective and/or underprotective and how it impacted your child. Discuss how you can learn to give the right amount of support.
2. What do you think about the concept of being centered in Christ? What biblical passages support this notion?
3. Why do you think we the authors pay so much attention to the relationship dimension? Do the child's mistaken goals make sense to you? Why is this important when it comes to communicating with your children?
4. The discipline dimension mentions several approaches that parents use to direct/control/guide their children. Why do we the

authors consider logical consequences to be empowering? What do you think?

5. Take one misbehavior that occurs in your home and come up with several logical consequences to deal with the issue. Practice how to deliver the consequence with your spouse or friend. How did you do?

6. Try having a weekly family meeting for one month. How will you introduce this idea to your kids? Evaluate how beneficial the meeting is after trying it for the month.

Part 2

Relationship Empowerment across Life Stages

5

And Baby Makes Three

Bonding and Belonging

The enduring affection and emotional bonding that forms between parent and child is the most essential element of parenting. When a tiny infant enters our world, the relationship dance begins. We engage and interact with our children from day one and throughout our lifetimes.

Each baby is unique and brings a unique challenge to us as parents. The labor and delivery are different. The circumstances of the adoption are different. Parents are different. Our temperaments and parenting styles influence how we interact. The relationship dynamics are set in motion and continue through a pattern of reciprocal responses through the life cycle. We are forever changed.

Our (the Pipers') children were born in very different circumstances. Aaron, the firstborn, had a difficult birth. While the first moments of life are usually noisy ones as the baby cries out in response to the harshness of its new world, Aaron's first moments were silent. He didn't breathe. The terror for us during that time was enormous. We had already lost one baby through miscarriage and knew of the possibility of not bringing this child into the world alive. Four, five, six, seven silent minutes passed, and finally Aaron screamed! We knew that the Holy Spirit had breathed life into him, and we were so grateful! But over the next few days as we marveled over Aaron, we were extremely attentive and anxious. I remember listening through the night to make sure he was breathing and watching him as he slept just to make sure he was okay. As a result, we tended to be overly protective of him during his first months, until we realized that he was going to continue breathing. He was our firstborn, so we had the freedom to be fully attentive to him. This can be a burden for a child. It took effort for Aaron to gain freedom from us and become the competent, independent young man he is today.

Karlie had an easier birth. Easier for her, that is. A few days after bringing Karlie home, Boni was taken back into the hospital because of extreme hemorrhaging. This meant Karlie was home, away from her mother during the first weeks of her life. While her father and brother were there to tend to her, it was just not the same without her mother. After several days in the hospital, Boni came home to a colicky, bottle-fed baby she needed to get reacquainted with. No sooner did that begin to happen, and war broke out in Cyprus, the country we were living in at the time. Boni left with the children in order to keep them safe from dropping bombs and bullets flying through our windows. Karlie was then separated from her father, who had cared for her when she had lost her mother. And external stress abounded for all of us! Aaron was old enough to know the danger that was present in those years of his life. He has grown into a serious young man with a deep sense of God's providence. Karlie, who was open to many people and knew no strangers as a young child, has become a woman full of adventure.

Sarah came to our home as a six-month-old baby of Korean origin. She came smiling by day and screaming by night! Knowing what we know now about attachment and bonding, we understand her screams and are thankful for her Korean foster parents whom she bonded with so well. Despite the cries, Sarah's brother and sister adored her and eagerly participated in her care. Sometimes they fought to be the one to feed her or have special playtime just with her. As parents, we were more laid back in our parenting, especially since she was a rather easy child. She felt loved by the four people in her family, as well as by her extended family and community, who had all waited so long for her arrival. Sarah has grown into a young woman comfortable with herself and with other people.

Relationship Empowerment

Erik Erikson (1963) considered developing trust to be the most crucial aspect of early childhood. He believed infants intuitively seek contact, and when parents learn the subtle innuendos of their babies' cries and respond accordingly, the babies learn to trust. When we hear hunger cries, we feed our babies; when they show signs of discomfort, we burp them; when they are sleepy, we rock them; when they are active, we give them stimulation, and so on. Consistent and prompt attention to a baby's needs establishes emotional and physical security.

John Bowlby (1979) was one of the first to pay attention to attachment and bonding between parent and baby. He surmised that the baby's coos, cries, and tendency to cling are instinctual in order to ensure survival. Following up with extensive research, Ainsworth (1978) noted the following three patterns of attachment: secure attachment, insecure attachment, and nonattachment. She discovered that when a new mother hadn't experienced a solid attachment to her own parents, she had more difficulty knowing how to make an attachment to her children. Early attachment experiences, it seems, determine a parent's ability to attach.

Secure attachment occurs when parents offer what babies need, when they are sensitive to signals for soothing, engage in loving interactions, and give stimulation that is "just right" for the babies. For example, an infant will turn his head away when he needs a break from stimulation. That's the signal for the mother to stop stimulating. If she overstimulates her baby when he needs quiet, he feels irritation and stress. On the other hand, if she doesn't pay proper attention, he won't get sufficient stimulation for healthy growth. This is why putting a baby on a rigid schedule and ignoring his cries runs counter to attachment theory. One baby may need frequent feedings for proper nourishment, while another does not. The hunger or discomfort cries indicate a need. Consistent, responsive care is the basis of secure attachment.

In a recent study, Sroufe (2000) found that by school age, children in the securely attached category were more cooperative with parents, more open to exploring their environment, and got along better with their peers. Children who could count on parents to be accessible in a consistent rhythm were able to manage their fears and stress better. On the other hand, when parents were unpredictable or unresponsive, children tended to be ambivalent about attachment, frustrated under stress, and had less capacity to keep relationships going with peers and parents.

After doing research on bonding and attachment in the Minnesota Study, Robert Karen (1998) reported that children with secure attachment histories scored higher in every area, from ego resiliency, to self-esteem, to independence, to the ability to enjoy themselves and respond positively to other children. These children were seen as having superior social skills—initiating more interactions with other children, sustaining them for longer periods, and, when approached, reacting with positive feelings. They also had more friends. Indeed, they held the majority of the top positions in popularity—an important finding in light of the fact that the degree of popularity among one's peers in third grade has been shown to be a strong predictor of emotional well-being in adulthood. The secure preschoolers also seemed to have more empa-

Responsive Parents Provide:

- A secure foundation of covenant love
- Steady, dependable responsiveness to child
- Availability—can be counted on to be there
- Accessibility—time and attention is given
- Warm, sensitive, loving response
- Protected, safe environment
- Joyful presence
- Soothing/calming presence during stress
- Ability to engage and disengage according to baby's needs
- Tender, enjoyable touch

thy for peers in distress. While children who were securely attached were not problem free, on the whole they were more competent, flexible, resilient, empathic, and had relational abilities to help them in trouble.

Bonding (secure attachment) forms the foundation of trust. As children soak in the safety of a predictable environment, they experience the world as a trustworthy place. The safety and security of parents' nurturing arms give children the confidence to reach outside themselves. Natural curiosity propels them to step into their intriguing world, but they know they can run back to the security of home base when things get a bit scary.

When Suzie crawls away from Mommy to discover new places in the house, all of a sudden she may realize that Mommy is out of sight. Frightened, she cries out, and Mommy comes to soothe her. She is comforted by physical contact. Later, she may only need to hear Mommy's voice from the next room to calm her fears. Soon, she figures out that parents can be counted on, even when they are not physically in the room, giving her the capacity to spend longer periods away from them. And she learns to keep them present internally. A transition object (security blanket, teddy bear, etc.) reminds her of the parents until they return home. Internalizing the parents in her heart and mind helps her during separations.

Fathers who bond with their babies at birth are profoundly impacted by the experience. Being present during the birth or adoption experience brings a deeply satisfying connection between mother, father, and baby. Fein (1978) found that the father's involvement in the birth process had a positive effect on his relationship with his wife and child. In addition, fathers actively involved in child rearing were more nurturing and sensitive in all relationships, according to a study by Russell (1978). An interactive effect is at work! Parents who make a space in their lives and hearts to bond with their infants will be well rewarded.

Difficult Bonding Experiences

Bonding doesn't come naturally for everyone. Think of Natalie, who is just sixteen years old. She has a baby conceived out of wedlock, and he often cries and demands attention. She tries her best to soothe him, but he still cries, making her feel incredibly inadequate. When she can't comfort him, she gets angry. Exasperated, she tosses him into the crib, and he screams even louder. The anxiety increases between them, and there seems to be no way of stopping the escalation. Natalie fears that, out of frustration, she will shake or spank the baby. And without some kind of intervention, this situation will go from bad to worse. Fortunately, interventions can be made to help young mothers like Natalie make that vital connection with their infants. And the sooner mothers like Natalie get help, the better. Currently there are therapies designed to help mothers learn how to attach to their babies.

According to Naylor (1970), there are three factors that determine a parent's capacity to bond:

- Quality of the parent's early experiences
- Conditions of the present situation
- Characteristics of the infant

We've discussed how parents' lack of attachment with their own care-givers makes it more difficult for them to attach to their children. In addition, the current level of stress in the lives of parents influences their ability to make good attachments. Whether it is family instability, marital discord, job insecurity, or health issues, such life circumstances deplete personal resources. A mother who is severely depressed or a father who has just lost his job will have a limited ability to attach, because they're focusing on themselves at the time.

The last factor in determining parents' capacity to bond is children who enter life under stressful circumstances. These children often require more from parents than those who enter life in ordinary ways. Premature babies and "at risk" births need special care even prior to birth. Toddler adoption has special challenges due to attachment or lack of it early on in life. Actually, when adoptive children experience grief at being placed with their new adoptive parents, this is a good sign. It means they have the capacity to make an attachment, even though it may take time.

Those toddlers who have not attached well may resist attachment or withdraw out of survival instincts developed in their orphanage or foster home. There may be sleep disturbances, fears, poor appetite, crying, withdrawal, or regression. In these cases, resistance or ambivalence about being comforted or cuddled can be expected. In fact, the child may show extreme behaviors such as rage, aggressive acts, negative, controlling behaviors, separation anxiety, and premature independence. But parents should hang in there! These children most likely will turn to them when they become a consistent, trustworthy presence. (Deborah Gray has given adoptive parents needed help in her book *Attaching in Adoption*. Her understanding of the attachment process for adopted children is a helpful aid for those families struggling in this area.)

I (Boni) had the wonderful experience of traveling to China with my friend Beth to pick up her adopted daughter, Maia, then fourteen months old. When Maia was handed to Beth, she screamed to go back to her caregiver. It was painful to watch her agony at letting go of the only caregiver she had ever known. Beth tried everything to comfort her those first minutes, with no success. I stayed in the background, handing Beth the bottle or diaper or Cheerios, in an attempt not to confuse Maia about who her mother was. Part of me was so glad she was protesting! In the middle of the night when she cried and cried and Beth despaired, we tried to remember how good it was that Maia was crying and missing her caregiver. In our exhaustion we would encourage each other by exclaiming, "She knows how to bond!" After a few days, Maia knew Beth was her new caregiver. She wanted Beth and only Beth after that. Aunt Boni was good for some fun, but Mom became her real joy!

For others, bonding doesn't work so easily. Many factors determine the seriousness of the inability to attach to new parents—how long the child was alone, what kind of care he or she received, prenatal conditions, and individual characteristics of the child, as well as many other circumstances that are part of understanding the level of attachment deficiency. While bonding capacity cannot be predicted with accuracy, it will be the first challenge and focus when bringing these toddlers home. Parents will need to focus on their role of fostering attachment, no matter how slowly it seems to develop. To begin with, parents must simply provide for the children's needs the way they would a newborn. Regressing behaviors (pacifiers, bottle feeding, frequent times of eating, etc.) may help the children cope.

Parents also will need to build attachment any way they can, such as offering a safe place to sleep, giving eye contact, responding with calm, soothing words, and showing empathy when fears occur. Morning and evening routines give structure so there is daily predictability, and weekly rituals provide a rhythm of regularly being with people or at events, such as church on Sunday or dinner with friends. Whatever creates a sense of belonging will help the process along. It's a delicate balance to be attuned to the attachment needs as well as developmental accomplishments. It takes patience, time, attention, and consistency.

We are persuaded that God created us with a built-in need for love and belonging. God is continually responsive and listens to and takes our petitions seriously. He hears us when we speak and stays intimately connected with us. This is a model for us to remain faithful when we are called to adopt a child.

Development Considerations

As a child moves from infant to toddler, the world seems to be theirs to explore. Their development in many different areas can be a wonder to parents.

Emotional Development

Toddlers are aware of themselves in a way that infants are not. Looking into a mirror, infants have no concept of what they're looking at, but toddlers will recognize themselves. At the toddler stage, children begin to distinguish themselves from others. For instance, when calling a two-year-old on the playground, you will see him respond by pointing to himself—"Here's Taylor!" In fact, toddlers are full of themselves! Me, mine, my toys! The toddler wants full attention, and learning how to share a toy or share a person is a huge challenge. Emotions like pride, jealousy, guilt, or shame have a self-conscious quality to them that is different from the infant emotions of happiness, surprise, fear, and anger.

Physical Development

Toddlers have learned many physical skills that separate them from infants. They jump, throw, run, climb, etc. They want us to watch and participate in what they do. "Throw football. Play house. Read book." Being allowed to do things on their own helps them develop feelings of accomplishment and pride, because they value their independence and want to be respected. This stage of life is also the time of the stubborn demands—"Me do it!" We as parents delight in all these accomplishments, but it takes our focus, time, and patience.

Language Development

Toddlers can use language to express themselves more fully. If a toddler feels shame for doing something she shouldn't have done, she may try to divert attention, hide, or avoid the situation. Children who are guilt oriented, however, will try to amend or fix the situation. How they respond is in direct relation to the parents' reaction. When children do something wrong, it's best for them to try to remedy the situation rather than hide. Affirm their honesty when they tell you what happened, and see if you can help them set things right.

Sexual Development

We are sexual beings from the beginning. At birth, babies have all the sexual apparatus that is needed for adult sexuality. Boy babies have erections, girl babies lubricate, and they both have pleasurable feelings in the genital area. Just as babies take pleasure in nursing, being touched, cuddled, and soothed, they are aware of and responsive to good feelings in many parts of their bodies. Of course, while young children experience pleasant sensations by touching their genitals, this is not to be compared with sexual arousal.

Parents who are comfortable with sexuality view sexual development as part of the whole picture. They are natural in responding to the nude body and help children be aware of all their body parts. Talking to toddlers about their penis or vagina (vulva) gives the children a feeling that all parts of them are acceptable, i.e., "Yes, that's your penis, this is your ear, this is your tummy," etc. Children usually feel no shame about walking in on anyone in the bathroom. This freedom makes bathroom behavior a normal part of life. After some time, your child may want privacy when attending to bathroom needs, and this is an opportunity to respect the concept of appropriate privacy.

When a child touches his or her genital area, this can be handled in a natural way by diverting the child or suggesting that this is something to do in private. In a matter-of-fact way, answer curious questions about sexual things, such as "Yes, boys have a penis, but Mommy does not have a penis. She has a vagina." Parents who affirm their children's bodies are more likely to give them a healthy start in accepting their sexual selves.

Discipline Considerations

Development Issues

What toddler doesn't want to get into drawers and strew everything across the floor, or dump out the entire toy box before choosing a toy? Young children don't yet have the concept of neatness, because they are in the process of freely exploring their environment and learning about it. A major part of raising children is being informed about age-appropriate expectations and behaviors. Punishing a child for doing things that are not part of their developmental level is a mistake many of us make. It's we who have a need for order, and while we recommend that our toddlers help pick up toys, the desire to be neat is not a natural inclination at this age.

There are excellent books (see appendix 2) written to describe what children are capable of doing at certain ages, with a range of competency. For instance, one child has better motor skills and can do more in the physical realm, while another child has early verbal skills but is clumsy. Understanding these differences helps us be flexible in our expectations and training.

The Scriptures listed below provide solid guidelines for training and disciplining children.

- Respect children as image bearers of the living God (Gen. 1:27; Ps. 8:4–8)
- Be sensitive to the unique needs of each child (Ps. 139:13–16; Matt. 10:30–31)
- Be wise in setting limits and guidelines (Col. 3:21; Heb. 12:5–6)
- Train and correct based on biblical injunctions (Eph. 4:26–32; 6:1–2)

Here the scaffolding principle applies. If we expect too much, too soon, this sets up unrealistic expectations that dampen and defeat. At the same time, insufficient stimulation or lack of belief in our children's abilities may result in underfunctioning. Toddlers are right on track developmentally when they assert their independence, demand attention, refuse to share, and even shout "No!" In these situations, we don't want to punish them for developing a self, yet they need guidance in learning acceptable ways of expressing their wishes. There are times when we should allow the assertion and patiently wait while they get themselves out of the car seat. On other occasions, we'll need to take charge and assist.

Spanking

To spank or not to spank. That is the question that often comes up for parents of young children. When it's difficult to communicate or reason with kids, sometimes spanking seems to be a reasonable option. We (the authors) remember reading Dr. Spock in our early parenting days, and his advice was to give kids a swift spank to the thigh with the hand, when other methods failed. In light of this, we'd like to discuss the biblical concept of "spare the rod and spoil the child."

First, let's consider that rod *(shebet)* is translated as staff, correction, or discipline. Proverbs 29:15 says the "rod of correction imparts wisdom." Discipline is done for training and correction so our children will gain an internal sense of right and wrong. Proverbs gives a strong admonition for parents to be discerning and wise, not hasty, angry, or hot tempered with children. Discipline is to be done out of love. First John 4:18 reminds us that there is no fear in love, because perfect love casts out fear. To "spare the rod and spoil the child" therefore means that parents must guide and direct their children. It does not in any way mean to beat them.

We should try to remember that shepherds used the rod to guide the sheep, not to beat them. Shepherds went to great lengths to protect the sheep and keep them safe. The image of Jesus as our Shepherd evokes a picture of one who goes to extensive measures to find and carry the lost or hurt sheep (us) back into the safety of the fold.

The beautiful passage of Psalm 23 refers to the Lord, our Shepherd, as one who provides, leads, restores, and guides. In fact, the rod and staff bring comfort and security and help us trust and hope in God during trouble. We belong to a Shepherd who searches us out and brings us back for our own good, out of love and interest, not out of anger or inconvenience.

Harsh discipline easily can dishearten our children and damage the relationship of trust and safety. But kind and firm discipline empowers. Deuteronomy 6:4–6 cautions parents to teach their children about God's way, out of our love. It requires living our lives morning, noon, and night, teaching our children about God.

Common Conflicts and Consequences

In this section, we'll look at some typical toddler behavior and offer some ideas about how to use appropriate consequences. There are several areas to keep in mind when disciplining toddlers. First, as we have stated, make sure that what you expect of them is age appropriate. Second, think also about what they might be trying to accomplish by their behavior. While we believe even small children are capable of doing wrong, we do not believe that it's our job to break their will. Hopefully our children will submit their will to God's will at some point in their lives and experience the discipline of bringing themselves under God's discipline.

Defiance

You ask Kelly, age three, to pick up her toys, and she turns to you and shouts "No!" Here are some things to remember:

- Kelly is capable of picking up her toys
- Apparently, Kelly doesn't want to pick up her toys
- Kelly is learning to assert herself

Remember that Kelly is learning the parameters of what is in her control and how to assert herself, what is allowed and what is not, and how relationships work. This helps you reframe "Kelly is being defiant" to "Kelly is experimenting." And that changes things from "You won't get away with talking to me that way, little girl!" to a more thoughtful "She's testing out her ability to say 'No' and needs to figure out the limits of what is allowed between us." Then you can get down beside Kelly, without anger, and say something like, "I know you don't feel like picking up your toys right now, but it needs to be done. Do you want to start with the dolls or the puzzle?" After Kelly begins, be sure to affirm her helpfulness.

Knowing that Kelly is developing a separate self should make it easier for you to keep your cool and not aggravate the situation or shame her. As toddlers experiment with their sense of self in these ways, giving choices helps. This affirms their self as separate from you as well as acknowledges that they have separate desires.

Positive affirmation is very effective at this age. You need to take every opportunity to affirm Kelly whenever she picks up her toys. And logical consequences should play a part as well. If Kelly continues to refuse to pick up her toys, you can bag them up and put them away somewhere, telling her, "These toys will be ready for you later, when you show you can pick up your toys tomorrow."

Temper Tantrums

Any child can throw a temper tantrum. It is something all parents dread, hoping and praying it doesn't happen in public. Here are some things to remember about temper tantrums:

- Don't try to reason with the child
- Don't have a temper tantrum yourself
- Keep your cool! Stay calm and nonreactive
- Decide where to deal with the tantrum

Tantrums rarely happen in isolation; an audience is part of the tantrum package. So remove the audience and decide where the tantrum can take place. It can be in the car, the child's room, a special place in the house—but make sure it's not a scary place. Settle the child down if you can. Remove yourself emotionally (don't take it personally) so you can be calm and firm. Walk away and let the child soothe himself or herself if you can't do it.

Then think about the situation and what caused him or her to go over the top. Were you in a hurry? Were you listening to the cues? Did you use harsh words? Was your child overly tired? Usually parents can predict what situations will bring on the tantrums, so try to avoid these situations and relationship dynamics. And when the tantrum is over, welcome the child back graciously by saying something like, "Oh, I'm glad you're done with that. I missed you!"

Dawdling

When Zach is refusing to finish his dinner so that you can't leave the house as planned, what do you do? First of all, let Zach know exactly when the family is leaving. If he continues to mess around, remind him that you are leaving as soon as the table is cleared and that you hope he doesn't have to go hungry. When the time comes, remove his food, saying, "I'm sorry you are going to be hungry during our evening together, but dinner is over. Time to get in the car." Don't take food for Zach, but don't belittle him either. Be matter-of-fact as you get him into the car for your evening activity.

Hitting, Biting, and Hurting Others

Biting and hitting is behavior that can never be tolerated in a child. Your little Meegan is a two-year-old, and her best friend, Tucker, is three months younger. While Meegan is generally a sweet little girl, she does have the habit of biting other children in her enthusiasm to get close to them. Tucker's parents get very upset with Meegan and with you whenever this happens.

In order for both children to be safe, you need to be very attentive during this biting and hitting stage. Since these behaviors normally are not done out of mean-spiritedness but instead out of exploration, action is the best course. Remove your child from the situation and point out the consequence of the behavior. "It's not okay to bite, so you must sit here away from Tucker for a while." Ask her to sit quietly and help her understand how the other child feels—"Tucker is hurt and crying!" If she is aware of his feelings and can say "I'm sorry," it helps her learn how to reconnect. However, if she gets up and intentionally bites again, you'll have to adjust the consequence, i.e., "We're going home, and you may not play with Tucker today." When she plays with Tucker the next time, carefully monitor her so you can quickly carry out the consequence if the action is repeated.

Toddlers are generally too young to play well together unsupervised. By keeping them in your sight and staying on top of their behavior, you can eventually stop bad habits such as hitting and biting. Toddlers generally outgrow this behavior as they learn how to be caring friends.

Whining and Complaining

The thing kids tend to remember about whining is that it works! We as parents can only take so much, and then we give in. For instance, two-year-old Jacob wants his pacifier, which he is only allowed to have in his bed. He fusses and whines and refuses to give up until you give it to him. Then he happily goes off to play, remembering that if he keeps up the whining, you will give in.

But if you are entirely consistent as a parent and never give in to whining, it will cease. This is the key. Don't give your child what he is asking for when he's whining. Calmly ask him to speak to you in a different voice. If he is even slightly able to do that, give him your attention. If not, walk away. Let your child know that you hear him, but that things will remain the same. In the case of Jacob, remind him that he gets his pacifier when he's taking a nap, distract him with something else, or put him and the pacifier in bed for a bit. If you give in and change the rules, it reinforces the idea that whining works.

Potty Training

Don't make a big deal of potty training, and it won't be a big deal! There is a time that's right for each child, so be alert for signs of readiness—i.e., the child stands in the corner to have a bowel movement. Since the child is aware of what's happening, you may encourage her to try the potty next time. Buying a special potty-chair, reading books on the topic, having her watch and help you flush the toilet helps her understand. Take advantage of nice weather and let your toddler play in shorts without diapers. This is a natural way to learn bladder awareness and control.

If your toddler is afraid of the big toilet or of flushing, you'll need to pay attention to his or her fears and find a way to alleviate them. Even something as silly as saying "Bye-bye to the poop" can give a lighthearted perspective. If your child tends to be constipated, he or she might find it difficult to relax on a toilet. If they fear it will hurt, they'll be reluctant to release. So pay attention to diet and make it easier for them. And help them feel proud of their accomplishment!

Parents Are Human Too!

What do we do when life circumstances crash in on us and we feel we can't cope? After all, it's not an uncommon thing for parents of young children to be overwhelmed, exhausted, and discouraged. The amount of time it takes to care for babies and toddlers leaves us feeling as if there is never time for ourselves. Fatigue, lack of sleep, and poor eating habits will burn us out fast. We must learn to take care of ourselves!

The toddler years are also a time when marital relationships may suffer. Maggi was so in love when she first married Chad. They were in their midthirties when they married, so they decided to have children a year after their "ideal life" as a newly married couple. Things happened quickly, and five years later they had three children under the age of five. Maggi confessed, "My children are hanging on me all day long, asking me to meet their needs. I'm exhausted! When Chad comes home, the only thing I want is a break and time for myself. It's hard for Chad to understand why I resist his sexual initiation, but I feel like it's just one more person who wants more of me than I have to give." Many mothers are able to identify with this. They are normal!

While a husband may hope for some romantic time with his wife, this won't happen when she is exhausted and overwhelmed. We've often heard about husbands who come home from work, eat dinner, read the paper, watch a game on TV, and then hope to have sex before falling asleep. The wives, meanwhile, who have been with the children all day, make the dinner, discipline the children, give baths, put the kids to bed after throwing a load of laundry in, and eventually crash on the sofa to rest their weary bodies. Sex is the last thing on their minds!

When a husband can see the bigger picture of what's going on with his wife, he can make a difference. If he takes over in the kitchen or spends time with the children so she can finish the meal, the evening starts out on a new note. Then when he pitches in to get the kids ready for bed, he gives his wife some time to relax. Honestly, this can make all the difference in the world. When a wife feels her husband is genuinely invested in her best interest and is participating fully in their lives together, she can focus on herself as a spouse. Then she can be open to thinking about time together as a couple.

Taking care of ourselves and our marriages is an investment of a lifetime. When we make plans as a couple, do meaningful, loving things for one another, and pray together for our children and each other, we not only boost our marriages but our family lives as well.

Spiritual Implications

The response to the first question in the Heidelberg Catechism ("What is your only comfort in life and death?") is a beautiful truth.

> That I am not my own,
> but belong—
>   body and soul,
>   in life and in death—
> to my faithful Savior Jesus Christ.

We belong to God. Isn't this an amazing truth? Isaiah 43:1 says, "Do not fear, for I have redeemed you; I have called you by name, you are mine." Even those who have not had a secure place within a human family can know what it means to belong to Christ. We are reminded in Psalm 100:3 that "it is he who made us, and we are his: we are his people, the sheep of his pasture."

God identifies himself as a mother who cannot forget her infant. Even if our human mothers forget us, God promises never to do so (Isa. 49:15–16)! God loves us and will be present with us for an eternity. "So, whether we live or die, we belong to the Lord" (Rom. 14:8 NIV).

Incomprehensible as it is, our salvation brings us into belonging with Christ. And if we belong to God and receive his loving response, how can we not offer a similar love and belonging to our children?

Reflection Questions

1. Take some time to think about how you bonded/attached to your parents. What did this mean to you and how has it impacted your ability to attach as an adult?

2. What do you remember (or what have you been told) of your early childhood? If you have a baby book, see if there are any clues in it, or ask your parents or other family members who can inform you.
3. What is it like for you to face your human limitations when parenting young children? Most parents are quite appalled at how angry they can get at their kids. What do you do at moments like these to keep from "out of control" actions?
4. How is this stage of parenting affecting you as a couple? What changes might be helpful in order for you to make your marriage more of a priority?
5. How do you experience belonging to God? Can you relate to the Isaiah passages? How does this impact your view of parenting?

6

Young Children

The Golden Age of Parenting

The golden years of parenting are usually met with great enthusiasm by parents. When our children reach elementary school age, their ability to care for themselves relieves us of hours of caring for them. In addition, our kids generally are enthusiastic and receptive to our input. This is a time to maximize social, psychological, and spiritual growth, because the basic attachment in the infant/toddler stage has laid a foundation of trust for this period of rapid development.

Children at this age master many life skills. New reasoning abilities are at their command. Competence is gained as they take on more meaningful tasks and develop work habits through projects and goals. In fact, developmental psychologist Erik Erikson (1963) identified initiative (ages four through six) and industry (ages seven through twelve) as the major developmental tasks of children. When children master these tasks, they establish a basis for continued growth in other areas. Doing their best and working toward specific goals becomes important to them for intrinsic reasons—they want to do well and work hard to make that happen. However, parents need to protect these enthusiastic children from overextending themselves. So before getting into the specifics in terms of what this age brings, we offer the following observation and caution.

We live in a world that can be a whirlwind for children. Gone are the days when a child comes home from school and spends the rest of the day playing with his or her friends. Today, many children need day planners to schedule all their activities! Playtime, if it's allowed, is even scheduled for them. In talking with a parent recently, we found that her third-grade daughter was scheduled from 6:00 A.M. until bedtime every day!

And this was the mother's doing, in an attempt to give her child all the advantages she'd never had. It's no wonder that the child has trouble with anxiety and experiences stress at this young age.

In *Time* magazine's article "The Quest for the Super Kid," the authors make this statement: "Kids who once had childhoods now have curriculums; kids who ought to move with the lunatic energy of youth now move with the high purpose of the worker bee" (Kluger & Park, 2001, April 30). What have we done to childhood? In an attempt to make sure our children are successful, we have eliminated relaxation and play. Kids are being treated like miniature adults who begin their formal education in preschool! The result of pushing for super kids is that children are suffering from "play deprivation." No wonder some children are worried, angry, stressed, or depressed.

Play with your children! Not the "gadget" sort of play that teaches them something or the side-by-side play of computer games but the old-fashioned play that develops a relationship. Read to your children, take walks, wrestle on the floor, finger paint and do something gooey. When it comes down to what children really need, the answer is "YOU!" They need parents who interact with them in playful ways. And they need this more than viola lessons and horse camp.

Kids also need time to *be*. To sit quietly. To relax. To notice nature. To be creative. To spend time with the family and friends. To laugh and have fun. Make sure your child is not overly scheduled and that the majority of their free time is time when they have access to you.

The thing that truly optimizes a child's potential is a trustworthy, secure relationship with the family. This happens naturally during family routines such as playing a game, talking in the car, engaging in activities, fixing a meal, or clearing away the dishes. No attempts at pumping up a child's IQ or giving "head starts" in extracurricular activities will contribute to a healthy well-being as much as spending time with you will. Of course, not all parents overprogram their children, and others fail to offer sufficient opportunities. We can fail on both ends of the spectrum. The main point is that what your children need most in life is time with you!

Relationship Considerations

The twofold goal of the REP model is to help children grasp who they are (self-concept) so they can find meaning in and through relationships, and to empower them to be competent, responsible human beings who contribute to the well-being of others.

Developing a Self-Concept

A child's self-concept refers to the sum total of the ways that child views himself or herself. When a child feels valued and is affirmed as competent, he or she takes on a competent identity. Having a positive self-concept does not mean a child is self-centered, however. In actuality, children with positive self-regard are more likely to reach beyond themselves to others.

Children of a very early age can grasp the idea of God's love. "Jesus Loves Me" doesn't have to be just a song they sing but something they can take deep into their hearts. Belonging to Jesus and being cherished as a child of God reinforces an identity in Christ. Internalizing the message that God has created them for a special purpose gives them meaning. And Bible stories about how Jesus regards children as precious invite them to come near to him. Just as children's self-concepts are formed in relationship to their earthly parents, so too must their identities be formed in terms of a personal relationship with God. This reinforces the doctrine of the covenant promises and the grace of God.

Sadly, some parents define God as one who disapproves of children. These kids tend to see God as an angry, punitive judge who is out to get them. I (Don) once heard a father say to his son, "God will throw you into hell if you disobey me." Unfortunately, this false picture of God is taken deep into a child's heart and self-concept as well.

Can you imagine what happens when Ben hears statements like "Boy, that was a stupid thing you did! What's the matter with you?" Or when Cindy hears "Can't you do anything right?" What do these comments do to Ben's and Cindy's confidence? Well, for starters, they begin to define themselves by these negative messages. The phrase "Nothing succeeds like success" can be reversed to "Nothing fails like failure." Such evaluative labels eventually bring about the expected behavior; it doesn't take long for Ben and Cindy to act accordingly.

An identity in Christ, however, gives the perspective that the self is defined by relational interdependence. To be able to think beyond the self, children need a strong awareness of a self that can give. In other words, those who have been valued will value others. Those who have been treated with respect will regard others with respect. Those who receive love will know how to show love to others. It is a reinforcing cycle of getting and giving.

When we let our kids know that we think they're great, they have an incentive to be great. Positive affirmation and acknowledgment of special qualities help them feel good about themselves. Hearing statements like "I really love you," "That was a very thoughtful thing you did," or "I really appreciate how you included your friend" gives self-confidence and self-assurance. There's a children's song that says, "I like you as you are, exactly and precisely, I think you turned out nicely, and I like you as you are." Isn't this the kind of message we want to give our children?

Here are just a few of the many ways that we can affirm our kids:

- Say something affirming every day
- Make positive comments about unique qualities of your child
- Notice Christ-centered behavior and comment on it
- Point out good effort and show appreciation for it
- Let your child know you approve of him or her
- Show interest in your child's world by working on projects together
- Listen and respond with empathy and emotional understanding
- Believe in your child

Developing a Personality

"Unique in all the world" are the words the little prince used to describe the rose he loved so much in *Little Prince* by Antoine de Saint-Exupery (1943). Isn't that an appealing thought? Don't we all want to be viewed as special people? Just think about it! God must take great delight in creating millions of people who are unique in every way. Even identical twins are different. God has created us with unique looks, talents, potentials, and beliefs. This is an astonishing truth!

Personality and temperamental differences help us see that there are many ways of being in this world. When we view differences as assets rather than deficits, we're able to take delight in each child's uniqueness. This keeps us from expecting one child to be like another. And when we view each child as special, this lessens competition and keeps us from setting up unrealistic expectations.

Different at birth and different throughout life, children give us important clues in how best to parent them. Also, personality inventories like the Myers-Briggs help us recognize just how differently people approach life and relationships. For example, some learn best by viewing things, others learn best using auditory means, while yet others learn best by hands-on experience. Some children are outgoing (extroverts), while others are more comfortable with internal processing of events (introverts); some do best through thought processes, while others use intuition to guide their way of being. The list goes on and on.

It is vital for us to know our children's learning styles so we can be "in sync" with them. When we use spoken words to teach a task to a child who learns best through audio means, she most likely will do the task well. Using the same method with a child who is visual does not work so well, since he learns best by watching how it's done. In his case, he does best when we demonstrate each step of the process.

It goes without saying that it's not only the children who are different. We as parents are different in how we approach life. The trick is to figure out how to honor the differences and work together as parents and children toward a deeper appreciation and understanding of one another. We need to be adaptable and creative in order to move with our children rather than against them.

It is a challenge for parents to approach differences with sensitivity and wisdom. While it may seem obvious that if you have a similar temperament as your child, you intuitively are more comfortable relating since you're familiar with how he or she works, this is not always the case. You may not accept a particular trait in yourself and therefore react to the child in a negative way.

When my daughter, Jacque, was about five years old, I (Jack) found myself introducing her (with chagrin) as "a little shy," while I proudly introduced my more gregarious son as "outgoing." One day it hit me that I was defining Jacque as a shy person and that this only reinforced her slight tendency in that direction. I had to confess that I was protecting myself from embarrassment when she didn't respond in the forward manner that I'd hoped she would. Because I've always struggled with shyness, I was supersensitive and even felt a sense of shame about being a shy person myself. But when I became aware of what I was doing and accepted her natural way of being with strangers, she was able to do just fine in making good connections with people.

Awareness is the key! We parents are aware of our own personality tendencies. Let's be alert to the unique traits of each of our children as well so we can be flexible in parenting them. This will pay great dividends, because children will feel valued and understood, just as we do when our uniqueness is accepted.

I (Judy) am an extrovert and learned through some painful mistakes to make adjustments in relating to my more introverted family members. I used to overwhelm them with my rather exuberant energy, but then I learned to hold back, slow down, pay attention, listen, and ask questions at a pace they could receive. Of course, that doesn't mean I had to dampen my personality completely—I know my family enjoys the energy and enthusiasm I bring to the home. Yet I learned to find an interaction style that enhanced rather than hindered the relationships with those I love. This has given me a new appreciation and respect for persons who come at life differently than I do.

Structure Differences

Some personality differences have to do with how much structure people prefer. Highly structured individuals are concrete and precise about the details of life and like to plan ahead. Less structured people are more relaxed about details and like to be spontaneous and keep their options open. Children of highly structured parents may feel inadequate when they aren't as orderly, while children of highly unstructured parents may feel at loose ends and need more clarity about rules.

You can see how a structured mother may have difficulty with an unstructured child. The mother may get frustrated trying to organize a child who doesn't naturally work that way. Even if she provides an organizer, it won't change his general way of approaching things. And it's just as disconcerting for a parent who is less focused to relate to a child who likes order.

So how do we give sufficient leeway to work with our children's natural styles? And how do we and our kids find a balance that helps them be effective within the limits of their personalities? First, consider the developmental capability, personality, and unique needs of each child. We should be adaptable and work for balance in our role as parents. For instance, a structured mother can decide to allow some nonstructure in her children's bedrooms, yet expect them to respect order in common areas of the home. A less structured father can develop routines to help his child more effectively focus on a task. Parenting according to the unique needs of our children models flexibility and acceptance. And it helps everyone in the family adapt to personality differences and function in a harmonious way.

God truly delights in diversity. Finding a right combination between personal preferences and natural differences is challenging, but working toward balance opens up possibilities for growth for everyone.

Sibling Differences

Can it be true that each of us wants to be the single focus of our parents' love and attention? While some may debate this sentiment, sibling rivalry goes back to the beginning of time, starting with Cain and Abel. So let's consider the impact of sibling position.

The child's position in the family (first, middle, last, only) influences him or her in various ways. Each sibling position holds universal characteristics that most of us can relate to. For example, the firstborn children are often achievement oriented and quite responsible. They are given special attention in the beginning and special responsibility later on. Middle children are often competitive in order to "catch up" to older siblings. They may look for a unique area of specialty to make them distinct. Middle children sometimes complain that they feel neglected or "lost" in a family or that they play a mediating role with siblings. Youngest children usually have been catered to by the family and tend to be laid-back and easygoing. The terms "baby" and "spoiled" are labels given to them by their siblings, but they usually are much loved by the family. Only children are similar in many ways to oldest children, but they have unique traits as well. They've had many privileges, similar to oldest or youngest children, but they tend to be quite adultlike in their attitudes and actions.

Children who come from large families tend to categorize themselves into groups. When there is more than six years of age difference between children in any family, they function as two separate sibling groups. This makes sense when you consider how things can change quite dramatically over the years within a family.

Whatever the situation, any position in the family has certain advantages and disadvantages. For example, if you are the only girl in a family of boys or the only boy in a family of girls, you may receive special treatment or get picked on. Also, there is great variability in how each family member responds to a new person entering the family, regardless of when that occurs. For instance, when a child is adopted into a family or when a family combines two sets of siblings (reconstituted families), or when a child is ill, has chronic disability, or dies, all siblings are impacted in different ways. Their age and position in the family determine how they incorporate such significant changes. It takes open communication and a sincere desire to work together around these sibling dynamics.

Here are some suggestions on ways to deal with sibling differences.

- Value each child's unique personality traits
- Make sure each child feels special and secure
- Respect the rights and privileges of each sibling position
- Appreciate unique contributions of each member of the family
- Discourage a competitive atmosphere
- Promote harmony and cooperation

Fairness within Limits

The familiar cry "That isn't fair!" lets us know that children are very aware of the concept of fairness. We must walk the fine line between being fair and deciding what's best for each unique child. Life, as we well know, is not always fair, so we need to resist falling into the trap of always trying to make it so for our children.

Certain decisions are right for a particular child for different reasons. If our children believe that we want what is best for each of them, they will usually accept a decision without complaining or feeling jealous. Hopefully, siblings will be happy when a brother goes to music camp, knowing that they can pursue other interests during the summer break. But we should be sure to listen when any child expresses feelings of being treated unfairly. It could be that one truly is being favored over another. Openly discuss this situation in a family meeting and make the needed adjustments. If each sibling feels a sense of worth and is acknowledged for their unique gifts, they most likely will cooperate because they don't have to compete to feel special.

Developing a Sexual Self

Curiosity is at the heart of learning, and we shouldn't be surprised that looking, touching, and playing are a natural way to learn. Children at this age explore gender and sexual differences in order to understand themselves, so questions related to sex and gender should be welcomed and answered. The relationship we've developed with our young children will pay off in this area. When children are secure in a relationship, they are able to talk freely about their behaviors and feelings. A calm responsiveness to their questions encourages them to keep asking.

Remember not to confuse adult and child sexuality. While a child may respond to self-touch with pleasure and giggles, arousal is not the goal. Some common behaviors at this age include kissing, showing each other private parts, using sex words that get attention, "I love you" notes, bathroom humor, and games. Children of similar ages may play doctor or touch each other's private parts in a way that should not be defined as erotic or abusive. They may feel excited or silly about what they're doing and even experience some pleasurable sensations, but they most often describe these feelings as weird or strange. When a parent walks in on such activities unexpectedly, the children may feel uncomfortable, wondering if what they are doing is bad. So don't reinforce this notion. Simply sit down with your child and explain that private parts are private and it is best not to show them to others. In most cases, when parents instruct children to stop sexual exploration, the behavior generally ceases, at least in view of the parents. But don't shame your child or make this experience more than it is. Set limits to behavior in a way that affirms their curiosity and sexuality and does not bring shame.

Communication

Inductive discipline (teaching/dialogue) is especially important at this developmental stage. It is a receptive time to talk about Christian values and how they impact decision making and personal choices. Our children want reasons for what we ask of them. A reasonable thinking process encourages them to take into account the effects their choices have on other people. And, most importantly, they learn this from how we communicate with them.

Communication (verbal and nonverbal) is the primary way we interact with school-age children and build their self-esteem. Affirm them in concrete terms: "Brendon, you do a real good job cleaning out the sink." Affirm new behavior: "I see improvement in your study skills." Give comments at unsuspecting times: "I love the way you make your brother laugh." Children gain so much from affirmation and validation.

And don't forget that communication includes listening. Listen carefully to what your children say and pick up on their nonverbal cues as well: "I notice you seem sad this morning. Is something bothering you?" Ask curious questions: "I wonder what made you so angry today after school?" Paying attention validates your children and helps them know you are genuinely interested.

Here is a specific illustration to point out the importance of listening. When eight-year-old Juan came home angry because he had been hurt by what his friend Reid had said to him, he needed to talk to someone who would listen. This was not a time for his mom to question, scold, or insinuate that he was partly to blame. Instead, she gave Juan a safe place to express his feelings. He knew his mom cared about him when she tried to put herself in his shoes as he unraveled the story. She helped him brainstorm ideas about what to do, and they rehearsed what he would say and how he would say it. Mom took the role of Juan's friend Reid and tried to anticipate some possible responses. All of this gave Juan the ability to decide for himself how he would handle the situation. Knowing his mother believed in him empowered him to act appropriately.

Common Conflicts and Consequences

As you approach areas of conflict between you and your children, ask these questions: "Whose problem is it and who needs to take responsibility for it? What natural or logical consequences can be useful in changing this behavior? Can I allow things to take their natural course and let the situation be the teacher?" Then make the decision to let your children suffer the consequence of their actions. This is the hardest part. Stay away from the trap of rescuing your kids. Let them face their teacher with unfinished homework. Let them wear dirty clothes when they fail to do laundry.

When we try to take responsibility for areas that our children actually control, we do them a disservice, frustrate ourselves, and create conflict in the relationship. Our task is to work ourselves out of a job by turning over to our children the things that are under their control. As children age, our responsibility for their actions diminishes, as does our control of their behavior. Our responsibility for their actions decreases proportionately to the actual control we have to make them do things. For example, our children must take responsibility for getting to class on time, doing their homework, being kind to their friends, etc. It is no longer our job to be in control of these areas. If we hold on to the fantasy that we are responsible for their actions, instead of turning things over to them, we develop a gap that creates conflict and anxiety for everyone.

In most cases, natural and logical consequences give us the edge in this struggle. There are many behaviors that can be handled quite easily with logical consequences. For example, not brushing teeth means they are not allowed to eat sweets; dawdling in the morning and being late for school means they must face school rules about being late and will have an earlier bedtime the next week; not caring for belongings means these things will be put away for a certain amount of time, etc. Most children understand this type of consequence because it is directly related to the behavior.

So put on your thinking hats as we consider the following common conflicts. We'll offer some ideas, but see if you can come up with your own creative consequences. Also, pay attention to how consequences help us let go and challenge our children to take control of their own actions.

Irresponsibility

Many parents complain of irresponsible behavior in their children. In an attempt to teach them responsible behavior, parents fix the problem for the child. The result is a belief that mom and dad will fix it, and the irresponsibility continues.

Let's presume the rule at your home is that only what's brought to the laundry room gets laundered. When Annie refuses to bring her clothes to the laundry room, she has no clean clothes to wear to school. This is her problem, so why should you get so upset? Actually, most parents get upset because they feel it reflects on them when their children wear dirty clothes to school. But in order to stop this behavior, you must let the logical consequences take their course. Do not make Annie's problem your problem. If you do, she will be forever irresponsible in this area, and you will be forever angry!

Other areas of irresponsibility might be forgetting their lunch, leaving their bike in the driveway, and losing things. The natural or logical consequences of these areas are obvious, but parents often cannot bear to have their children experience them, so they bring a lunch, move the bike, look for the lost sweater. And they rescue, nag, and shame. Children go deaf to the nagging but never change their behavior.

So let the consequences do their work and don't hinder the process. Your kids will never learn different behavior if there is no consequence to suffer. If they have to go hungry during lunchtime, do without their bike that is put away for a week, or spend time looking for their lost sweater, they begin to learn from the mistake.

Rude Behavior

A typical complaint of parents is that their children lack respect. But in working with families over the years, we've been amazed at how many parents talk disrespectfully to their children. So first, check your behavior toward your child. Rarely will children be disrespectful when they're treated with respect. However, sometimes rude behavior has been tolerated, and a habit forms that needs to be broken. Parents' consistent refusal to tolerate the behavior is a first step in learning respect.

Look at this example. The Holstine family had planned to go out to dinner to celebrate the end of the school year. But they feared that their fourth-grade son, who had been giving them problems recently, might sabotage the time together. So they planned ahead. Sure enough, Jimmy didn't like the place they had chosen and began talking about how lame and dumb his parents were. So his dad calmly told him that the family would be leaving, but he wouldn't be going with them. The neighbors would look after him, so he could grab a bowl of cereal before heading over. His dad then said they were sorry not to have him along, but they knew he wouldn't have a good time anyway. "See you when we get back, son. It may be late because we may take in a movie. But don't worry, the neighbors said you could lay on their couch till we get back." And off they went, out for a great evening. Jimmy was stunned! He hadn't gotten the fight he'd been expecting. What he learned was that his behavior would not control the family. As a result, he realized that his parents had other options and that disrespectful behavior would not be tolerated.

Sibling Fights

It is painful for parents to observe their children fighting. We desire for them to act lovingly toward each other, and when fights erupt, it is upsetting. The temptation is to get into the fight ourselves, which usually makes things worse. While it may be their desire to draw us in and get us to take sides, that will only escalate the problem. Children can learn to be responsible for the conflicts between each other.

A friend told us of a difficult situation in her family. When the children were ages six, ten, and twelve, they constantly fought in the backseat of the car. Marsha had tried several things to stop this behavior, but nothing worked. Her son in particular seemed unwilling to give up the fight. So one day she decided to do something different to let them know the behavior was not acceptable. Since these fights mostly took place on the way home from school, she planned ahead. As they were riding home and the fighting began, Marsha calmly told the children that she would not tolerate fighting in the car while she was driving and that if they wanted a ride home, they needed to stop immediately. Perhaps because of her unusually calm voice (these fights normally made her take on the destructive behavior of her children), the girls settled down.

Sam, however, escalated his behavior and continued to torment his sisters. So Marsha pulled the car over and told him he would have to walk. He stared at Marsha in disbelief, since they were more than a mile from home. She reminded him that he needed to walk straight until he came to their street, and that she would see him later. He got out with a sneer, thinking there was no way his mom would leave him, but away she drove. Marsha's friend Marty, who was following her in her car, later reported that Sam stood for a long while waiting for his mom to come back and get him. When twenty minutes had passed and Marsha still hadn't shown up, he began walking, not knowing that Marty was following him to make sure he arrived home safely.

Sam came in the house tired and quiet, and Marsha welcomed him home with no lecture. That experience ended the sibling fights in the car. When a skirmish started, she simply asked if anyone preferred to walk home. Sometimes it takes a jolt to change a behavior that we have tolerated too long.

Homework Hassles

Homework is one area of control that parents find quite impossible to give up, probably because it has to do with their children's future success. However, the first thing to remember is that it is their homework!

It is their future! Of course, you're invested in their success, but you can't do their homework for them. You can't force them to learn. It's their responsibility.

By fourth and fifth grade, children generally can be in charge of their homework. Stay out of it! Let homework be between your children and their teachers, and let your children pay the consequences of not completing their homework. Of course, you should always be available to help with homework if asked. But remove yourself from the job of making sure it gets done.

If they do not take responsibility for their homework, you might explain to them that the goal is for them to do it without pressure from you. Perhaps they are not ready for the responsibility, so you may agree to monitor the homework for a month. Spend scheduled time teaching your child good homework habits (setting up a place to work, turning off the TV, setting a specific time of day to do it, etc.). In other words, for that month, they do it your way. After that, turn the task over to them. Children usually want this responsibility for themselves; it feels better than having parents dictate to them. But sometimes they need to see the alternatives clearly before they take on the task.

TV

As a family, you will want to set guidelines for how much TV your children may watch. Be consistent and don't be afraid to be different from the parents of their peers. The goal is to teach your children to monitor their own behavior. Watching TV programs that you specifically forbid means they are not monitoring their behavior, so a logical consequence would be no TV for a period of time.

Bedtime

Bedtimes are for your children's health and often for your mental health as well. Don't be afraid to be consistent here; children naturally

---

Homework Hints

- Believe in your child's ability to take charge of homework
- Provide study-skills guidance, time, and place to study
- Help when asked
- Don't nag
- Affirm, affirm, affirm!

will want to push the limits as much as possible. Your job is to make sure that push is the exception and not the rule.

You can't make your children fall asleep, but you can insist that they be in bed at a certain time. It's okay for children to have time alone in their beds before falling asleep. They may use this time to reflect, pray, or read. You don't have to be responsible for making them fall asleep. However, their mood the next day or their inability to get up in the morning may mean that the logical consequence is an earlier bedtime. Be matter-of-fact and stay out of power struggles.

Allowance

This is a good way to teach children responsibility with money. They can also learn the blessing of tithing, buying gifts for others, and saving for things they want. Conflict usually arises when parents want to control how children use this money or how much is appropriate for the child. I (Boni) have heard children argue in therapy sessions that fifty dollars a week is not enough, while others try to get a raise from two dollars.

Decide what is the purpose of the allowance. Are they buying clothing and school supplies or just fun stuff? Is there a part of the money that is totally at their discretion for spending? How will raises be calculated? Do older children get more than younger children? Does more responsibility in the household mean more money for allowances? Are there other ways to acquire money if the child wants to earn it? Being clear in this area will prevent conflict.

Be Merciful as God Is Merciful

When natural consequences are difficult to bear, sometimes it is appropriate to ease the burden that childish decisions have created. I (Don) learned mercy from my father in many ways, but one particular day stands out to me. As a young boy, I had taken on the job of raking my neighbor's leaves for the sum of five dollars. I had to get all the leaves in the yard raked before I could receive the money. But after a while, it was early November and the leaves were still falling from the trees. I found myself raking leaves from morning until night. As one area became free of leaves, the next area became full. As the afternoon wore on, it got colder and darker, and discouragement was setting in. I could hardly lift my rake. I wasn't expecting any help because I knew it was not my parents' responsibility to bail me out of a situation I had created.

Yet just when I was at my lowest point, I looked up and saw my dad coming down the street with rake in hand. He walked up to me and asked if I could use some help. I thought my heart would burst with gratitude. I became encouraged and invigorated. The burden was lifted, and in a short time we finished the job and went home together in the dark. My dad was not obliged to help, and I knew it. He had acted in grace and mercy. And I never forgot it. My dad modeled God to me in a profound way that day.

Let's never forget that one of the greatest gifts we can give our children is an understanding of God's mercy. It is always a balance to know when to allow our children to suffer the consequences of their actions and when to step in and offer mercy in some way. A child growing up with no consequences will not understand the call of Christ to obedient life in the Holy Spirit. However, a child growing up without mercy will have trouble understanding the freedom from sin and guilt that Christ offers. God is our example; discipline *and* mercy are crucial for responsible living and for maintaining our relationships.

Parents Are Human Too!

What we model has a powerful influence on our children. Values, faith, and morality are transmitted through what they see in our lives. When we are loving and respectful, it rubs off and is sought out. However, since we are human, we will not always parent perfectly. There will be discrepancies in what we say and do. We will make mistakes, just as our children make mistakes. But acknowledging our wrongdoing, asking forgiveness, and changing our behavior will also have a tremendous impact. Just as we face consequences for our sins, God draws us back into his loving arms so we can receive forgiveness and reconciliation. Forgiveness is the most important thing we can model for our children. It keeps us humble and relationship minded.

Spiritual Implications

God in his great mercy does not always give us what we deserve. In fact, rarely do we suffer the full consequences of our sins. In God's mercy, Christ steps in to take the punishment for the sins we commit. We get ourselves into all kinds of situations that God in his justice could strike us dead for. But God is not only just, he is also loving and merciful. Let us never forget this as we attempt to teach our children and model Christ to them.

Reflection Questions

1. What are the personality differences in your family, and how do you manage them? Is it easier for you when you're similar or dissimilar to your children? Why?
2. What was your sibling position in your family? How did it impact you? Were there unique family circumstances that had an effect on your sibling relationships? How can you be more sensitive to your children in terms of their sibling positions?
3. What logical consequences have been effective in your family? Discuss what you did and explain why it worked so well.
4. Share an issue that is a current conflict in your home, like doing family chores. Brainstorm "fitting" consequences that may be effective. Put into practice one consequence and see how it goes. Review what happened.

7

Preteens

Challenge and Competence

In the Jewish tradition, the Bar or Bat Mitzvah is the religious ceremony that acknowledges when a child has become an adult. At twelve years of age, the young person stands in front of family, friends, and the entire community of faith to read the Torah. And when the reading is over, the rabbi pronounces "Now he is a man!" or "Now she is a woman!" Even though some in the audience may quietly chuckle under their breath at the pronouncement, the preteen is awarded adult status.

Though twelve years old seems a bit young to transition into adulthood, kids in today's world seem to be growing up faster than ever before. The transition is usually an awkward, in-between phase of life. One parent made this comment: "It happened virtually overnight! Our obedient, kind, affectionate child turned into a surly, defensive, and defiant teenager."

We've heard it said that you either love middle school kids or you hate them! Very few people are neutral about children this age. Our (the Pipers') daughter Karlie recently finished her training as a middle school teacher. When people would ask her what age group she wanted to teach, they'd often think that they'd heard wrong. Surely not middle school! Not the preteen group that everyone fears and few understand!

But that is only half the story. Many preteens have an innocence about them that makes teaching an exciting venture. They are capable of thinking about significant matters and aren't too cool to express their thoughts. Being seen with their parents is still an okay thing, and family life remains a priority. But while some draw close to family, others stretch their wings into a world consumed by peer relationships.

What we see in preteens today, we saw in adolescents thirty years ago. The problems I (Boni) saw when I taught in high school are now problems my daughter sees in middle school children. Our kids move ahead at an earlier age than past generations, yet the basic needs of this group are no different from the past. Preadolescents need us to stay connected, even though they are learning how to be independent. No matter how hard they push, most have mixed feelings about leaving childhood behind. This is what makes life so crazy and confusing. So in spite of the irritation this age group can cause, we should think beyond the changing moods and extreme behaviors to the relationship. Their mental health and ours depend on it.

Developmental Considerations

Autonomy and Ambivalence

As your preteen progresses from dependency to independence, ambivalence is normal. At one moment they may resort to childish ways, and the next moment they may leap into sophistication beyond their years. Sometimes they may back up a step or two out of deep-seated insecurity about what's expected of them. Being aware of the vacillation helps us guide and support them through these vulnerable times of change, because they may be doubtful whether they can make the transition. A cartoon depicts this thought well. A preteen is lying on her bed, talking into a tape recorder. She says, "Parents are so dense! Don't they know that all I want them to do is to take care of me and leave me alone?" This sums it up nicely! But how do we take care of them *and* leave them alone?

I (Judy) remember asking "Where did my little girl go?" when my twelve-year-old daughter and I went shopping for a winter coat one year. Jacque selected a long, elegant, fur-trimmed coat from one clothes rack while I came up with a cute, red embroidered one from another part of the store. Obviously there was a clash in our minds about how "grown up" she was. I quietly put the coat I had picked back on the rack and applauded her for finding such a beautiful coat. That was a day when I needed to give up on keeping her young and to support her desire to be more grown up.

Giving lots of room for fluctuation as they move between dependence and independence is so important. But a stable presence is also crucial. Letting them know that they can count on you when the going gets tough gives them courage to maneuver through stormy times. Your connection and belief in them will help them stay afloat until the winds calm down and the water becomes more smooth. They are right on track developmentally, so hang in there with them. Soon they will move into the more consistent teenage stage.

Thinking for Self

Preteens are more likely to ask "Why not?" than "Why?" They want to make decisions for themselves. They have minds of their own and will test your reasons and values. They will look for alternatives and want a say in family decisions. Increasing their involvement in family meetings, trying out their ideas, letting them have a voice in problem solving, and trusting them to make good choices will keep them involved in family life.

Expectations

Expectations "two sizes too big" can cause havoc with preteens. They are easily overwhelmed by standards they feel are beyond them. Falling on one's face is to be avoided at all costs. Since they are afraid of failure, they are more likely not to try at all rather than try, fail, and be criticized. Any unnecessary humiliation, during a time when uncertainty is the predominant experience, only discourages them further. So keep your expectations in line with their unique abilities and maturity (as we mentioned in the scaffolding discussion in a previous chapter).

Mood Changes

Physical and hormonal changes often lead to mood swings that can be unsettling to preteens and parents alike. Virtually every one of them wants to know if they are normal. So keep in mind their overwhelming need for peer approval and acceptance. They will no doubt check things out in detail and spend hours on the phone getting advice from friends on any number of topics. They may not come to you as much for advice. They may have more difficulty trusting your judgment, even though they also have trouble trusting themselves as well. In fact, they may seem to flip from one emotional extreme to another.

You may find it difficult to make yourself available when they give you the cold shoulder one minute and demand your undivided attention the next. But while it's easy to feel jerked around by their emotional state, you need to hold steady and stay in balance. Your nonreactive presence and patient interaction through the ups and downs of their world is reassuring to them. Stay as connected as they'll allow.

How to Promote Healthy Sexuality in the Home

- Be ready to discuss any questions regarding sex
- Respect privacy (dressing, sleeping, bathroom use, nudity)
- Set comfortable, age-appropriate physical and emotional contact
- Respect boundaries (knock before entering)
- Promote group socializing and friendship versus one-on-one dating
- Affirm bodies as beautiful and unique
- Endorse God's good gift of sex
- Encourage physical activities that build body confidence

Sexual Development

While not quite at full steam, the hormones are flowing and body changes are noticeable. Voices are lowering, pubic and underarm hair is developing, breasts are budding, menstruation and wet dreams are occurring. These biological changes leave preteens feeling awkward and squirrelly about their bodies. Yet they are acutely aware of their newly discovered sexual self.

With the first menstrual cycle for a girl and first ejaculation for a boy, pubescence has arrived. They are now capable of reproduction! You may wonder how to talk about these sexual changes and what they might mean. One mother reported that her daughter literally turned cartwheels in the living room when she tried to talk about sex, screaming, "I don't want to hear about it!" Obviously this child was not ready to have a discussion. Pay attention and bring up the topic when your kids are open to it.

The onset of menstruation can be a time to affirm a daughter's "coming of age." While some families celebrate the event by taking their daughter out for a special dinner or giving her a bouquet of flowers, in other homes daughters don't want to make a fuss and parents aren't informed until well after the fact. Boys generally do not disclose having their first wet dream, perhaps out of shame or a desire for privacy. So be alert and sensitive to your children as you help them come to terms with the sexual changes. Hopefully, a comfort level has been established so that when they're ready, you can talk openly about the changes that are happening in their bodies.

Some parents tend to hold back from showing physical affection to preteens because they are conscious of their children's budding sexuality. Just when preteens need acceptance and affirmation of their sexuality, their parents get uneasy or uncomfortable. So find sensitive and appropriate ways to give a hug. Think about how you can make affirmative comments about their bodies such as "You're building great muscles in your workouts!" or "I've noticed how agile you are when you run track" or "The way you take care of your skin is really paying off."

In this day of media exploitation, we should monitor our children's intake of sexual material and be aware of what we watch when they are around. Late elementary-school age is not too early to teach children to be critical consumers of television and other forms of popular culture. For instance, when your preteen boy pays special attention to a commercial featuring a seductive young woman in tightly fitting clothes, you might point out how sexuality is being used to sell a product. Or when coercive sex is depicted on television, you might use the situation to make comments such as, "Men shouldn't force women like that; it's not how God wants us to treat each other." Ask your children what they think about what's being portrayed and use it as an opportunity for open discussion. Take time to talk about something they don't understand. Look for teachable moments about how God wants us to regard values about sexuality and human relationships.

Acutely aware of sexual risks, parents understandably want to protect their kids from premature sexual encounters, unwanted pregnancies, and sexually transmitted diseases. Indeed, these are life-changing and life-threatening concerns, and parents want to do whatever they can to keep their kids from such vulnerable situations. So be on the alert for involvement in chat room activity, pornographic materials, access to alcohol or drugs, unsupervised one-on-one boy/girl interaction, even in your own home, etc. Be clear about your expectations concerning unsupervised parties and let them know you'll come to get them should they ever find themselves in a precarious situation.

Combat the predominant cultural promiscuous-sex messages with a biblical person-centered view of sex within the confines of marriage. Teach them how to assert themselves in boy/girl friendships. Build their self-confidence and strength of character so they will be able to resist the crowd and stand firm in their convictions. Be realistic with them about the worldly view of sex. A friend of ours bluntly told her daughter, "Most boys this age do not want a relationship but simply want to take your clothes off and have sex!" A father may remark about the demeaning messages in the media that treat women and girls as sex objects. A mother may respond to her son's offhand comment that "women say 'no' but mean 'yes'" by clearing up this common misperception, letting him know that what women really want is a trustworthy, secure commitment from a man. Don't be preachy but have an honest interaction about the important topic of sex.

Here we list some of the variables related to early sexual involvement to help you determine the needed guidance and boundaries for your preteens (Chilman, 1980).

- Low level of religiousness
- Permissive social norms
- Peer-group pressure
- Use of drugs/alcohol
- Risk-taking attitudes
- Going steady/being in love
- Low self-esteem/desire to be loved
- Aggression/proving manhood
- Early puberty

Note the importance of religion. Being part of a Christian youth program (peer influence) and being loved by members of a church is a proactive way for preteens to find values and strength from their faith. Make sure you offer positive messages from a biblical perspective, such as "God created us as sexual beings for a deeply satisfying, person-cen-

Essentials of Preteen Sexual Morality

- A clear sense of belonging to family and faith community
- A clear sense of assurance about what's right
- A value system that determines behavior
- An ability to say "no" to peers who pressure
- A sense of competency and comfort about one's body
- Self-discipline and "other" focus
- A positive view of sexuality as a God-given gift

tered relationship with a future spouse." One preteen told me (Judy), "I don't just want my parents to tell me all the bad stuff; I want to hear about the good part of sex too." While links to peers are strong during this stage of life, so are the links to you, your family, and your faith community. Placing sexuality in the context of a lifelong, monogamous, covenant relationship gives preteens a solid reason for their beliefs and behaviors. Well-informed young adults can stand on the strength of who they are in Christ with the support of family, friends, and church.

Personality Differences

In the previous chapter, we discussed how personality differences impact family relationships. By now, these differences will be ingrained into your children's unique personalities. Your daughter may be talkative, spontaneous, and stubborn, while your son is quiet, keeps to himself, and never causes a problem. She likes to break convention, evident in her style of dress and radical ideas, while he is more conventional and rarely shares what he's thinking. In both cases, you'll need to respect their ways of being. If you try to change her, she'll rebel; if you intrude on his private space, you'll alienate him.

Janice, a single mom, had different responses to her two preteens. It was easy with Alexis, who was similar in personality to Janice, and they enjoyed talking, laughing, and being emotionally close. But her relationship with Justin was more difficult, since he was high strung, a worrier, and more serious about life. Janice didn't have a clue how to relate to him. At times, she resented him for "dampening" the atmosphere in their home.

After attending a workshop on personality differences, the light went on for her. Once she understood and acknowledged the differences in her two children, new possibilities opened up for the family. After Justin felt her acceptance of him, he could relax and lighten up a bit. Janice found ways to interact with him through common interests, and this became a bridge between their differences.

In another family, Jerry, the father, had a higher need for structure than his kids. He requested that the dishwasher be packed in an orderly fashion. Once the kids heard the "rhyme and reason" behind his desire and understood his need for efficiency, they willingly honored his wishes. It was a reasonable request, but more than that, they knew it mattered to him. In turn, he was able to be flexible about how they kept their rooms.

The idea is for the family to find creative ways to deal with differences. In doing this, a distinction can be made between personal preferences and deeply held values. Each family member should stretch beyond their comfort zone in order to accommodate others. This will then be a growing edge for everyone and keep interdependence as the focus.

Relationship-Empowerment Dynamics

As your children reach preteen years, you may assume they don't need as much affection. Nothing could be further from the truth! You may conclude that they are confident of your love; after all, you sacrificed for them in many ways during the early years. To consider that your love may be questioned at this point may come as a shock. But the fact remains that kids never lose the need to know they are loved. So let them know you love them in a variety of ways—a warm hug, an expression of affirmation, an appreciation for something they've done, an evening spending time doing things they enjoy.

Mothers and fathers may express affection differently. Mothers are more likely to be equally affectionate with daughters and sons, giving hugs and verbal expressions of love. Fathers seem to be more able to show affection to daughters and are apt to do things with sons that focus on masculine identity as a way to show affection. In general, preteens may shun physical expressions of love by parents, especially in public. Increased need for privacy is natural, and we must respect their wishes. However, acceptable expressions of love in the privacy of the home usually are quite acceptable. There are also times when preteens distance themselves from us, and it's hard to know how to break through this barrier. At these times, we should wait it out but continue to make ourselves accessible. Once sufficient independence has been established, preteens can let down the barriers and be receptive to us again.

Communication and connection go hand in hand. No matter how good the connection of earlier years, parents will need to make concerted efforts to stay connected with their preteens. You may be saying, "We sure blew it! We didn't establish an atmosphere of open communication when our children were younger. Now that they're older, there's nothing we can do!" But this isn't true. It is always worth doing whatever you can to make a connection. It's never too late! While we can't change our preteens, we can change ourselves—and this will change the interaction.

Even though it's sometimes hard to understand the preteen world, more than anything, kids want to be understood! Find natural opportunities to listen, whether it be riding in the car or fixing a meal together. Be genuine! Preteens hate anything fake. If you listen halfheartedly, out of a sense of parental duty, they will stop talking. Don't be intrusive with questions, but find a way to be curious and interested in their lives.

After our (the Balswicks') son Jeff died of cancer at age nine, Jacque, age eleven, dealt with her grief privately. A few years later, in anticipation of entering her second year of junior high school, Jacque made the casual comment, "Gee, Mom, if Jeff were alive, he would be in my school this year, and I'd be showing him all the ropes." Judy's ears heard the words but also listened for what Jacque was saying behind the words. She responded, "I guess it makes you feel cheated out of a special role in his life. That must really hurt!" This created an opportunity for Jacque to express more of her sadness over Jeff's death. This is an example of

Communication Tips

- Be honest, straightforward, and direct
- Stay calm when their emotions explode
- Be clear and reasonable in your stance
- Stay interested in their world, what they say, how they think
- Empathize with their feelings
- Keep confidences
- Listen, listen, listen

picking up on natural conversation and taking it to a deeper place. Avail yourself of every opportunity by listening for an opening.

Making Choices

Of course we all hope our preteens will make choices in line with Christian values and principles. But there may be times when our basic beliefs are at odds with those of our children. While we are obliged to express our concerns, we must be careful to engage in respectful dialogue. When there is an impasse, it may help to bring in an objective person outside of the family.

During junior high school, I (Judy) and my parents were at an emotional deadlock. My parents disagreed with the spiritual practices of the church I was attending. The heated argument between us became so strong that we could not get through it. A gentle, caring pastor in the community came to our family at this time of turmoil. He provided a safe place for me to express my enthusiasm about the church and also helped me listen to my parents, who wanted me to worship with them. Without dampening my spiritual life, the pastor helped us find an acceptable resolution. In essence, he brought a healing light to a dark situation. When we could listen to each other with respect and compassion, my parents and I could get back to the love that was behind the heated issue between us.

As we work out differences with our preteens, it is imperative that both sides give up idyllic expectations or defensive postures. When we hear each other out, step back from our biases, opinions, and fixed stances, we can listen with understanding. Sometimes, out of our desire to have our children turn out a certain way, our vision is clouded. Finding creative alternatives will bring back balance to the relationship.

There are other times, however, when we must risk our discomfort and challenge our teens' behavior. When this happens, we should be honest and direct as we work through the rough places of disagreement. We should also be ready and willing to give input that stretches their thinking and expands their views. Demanding compliance without explanation only results in rebellion or rejection of our ideas. So we should be careful to reasonably offer our viewpoints with the hope that our children will be able to integrate our input.

Anger

Anger is the common emotion that comes up between preteens and parents during conflict. You may wonder if anger is okay. If so, what kinds of expressions of anger are acceptable? What we believe about anger determines how we will deal with it in our homes. If we believe it is an act of disrespect, we'll take it personally. On the other hand, if we believe it is a God-given emotion that alerts us when something is wrong, we'll want to understand what it's about. Let's take a look at ways people deal with anger.

Deny/Repress

Those who believe anger is bad have a tendency to repress any inkling of this emotion. They deny their anger or keep it inside where it can boil into something even more extreme, like rage, hate, or self-loathing. This anger can be directed toward and take a toll on the self (eating disorders, physical problems, drug abuse) as well as on relationships.

Suppress

Sometimes people choose to suppress anger. This means that they are aware of the anger but choose to put it aside for a variety of reasons. Often they find alternative ways to release the energy, like going for a jog, cleaning the house, talking to a friend, etc., until they can deal with it more directly. Maturity helps people find appropriate ways and means to resolve anger. If they can't deal with it directly, they must find a way to put it to rest.

Express

Anger can be expressed in negative or positive ways. Some people are verbally and physically abusive while expressing anger, which is damaging to those around them. However, listening to the anger can help people determine the deeper meaning and find an opportunity to express it in a way that "rights a wrong." It can empower them to acknowledge what's happening so they can work on the relationship issues.

Beneath Your Preteen's Anger

Anger is often a reaction to being misjudged, misunderstood, ignored, undervalued, or mistreated. There is usually some kind of hurt or fear behind anger; many interactions happen each day that can cause preteens distress and anxiety. There is a lot at stake in their world of competition, and parents can help them learn skills to sort out anger, fears, and insecurities.

Look for the "hidden" feelings behind the anger, and you'll be ahead of the game. An expression from your preteen like "I hate my teacher!" can elicit from you a lengthy diatribe about having respect for teachers. Your child then gets lost in the midst of the lecture. But listening to her feelings and having empathy about what happened that day can lead to a different response. Perhaps she was humiliated in class or embarrassed by a bad grade. Anger can cover feelings of humiliation or fear. So by being attentive, it's possible to address the real problem.

But what if the parent is the object of the anger? What if the "I hate you!" is directed toward you! Then it's twice as hard to stay objective and nonreactive. Now is the true test. Take a deep breath and resist the temptation to be retaliatory. Instead of countering with indignation, which swiftly shuts up your teen, you may choose to say something such as "Boy, you're really angry with me right now, and I feel the heat. Let's talk about what's going on a little later when we can be calm. I want to know why you're feeling so strongly about this." Dealing with angry feelings in a constructive way teaches preteens how to deal with others in like manner.

Parents have feelings too! You should also be able to admit your feelings of anger with your children. Let them know you were hurt by a comment or sorrowful about a lack of connection. Your vulnerability will show them you are human too. Also, don't be afraid to ask for forgiveness when your behavior is inappropriate. For instance, you might have gotten upset at work and lashed out at your child when you got home. Saying something such as "I'm so sorry I took out my anger on you—you didn't deserve that" models humility and is an example of how to mend relationships after a disruption.

Discipline Empowerment

Before our children reached the preteen stage, we were pretty much responsible for controlling what they did. This becomes less and less true with preteens. Many of us have difficulty giving up responsibility for things we cannot control. This creates a huge amount of stress. In chapter 6, we concluded that parental responsibility and control must be diminished concurrently as children become in control of and responsible for themselves. If we insist on trying to take responsibility for things we cannot control, we will live in a household full of conflict.

There are too many disagreements between parents and preteens, so pick your battles carefully! Decide which areas to ignore and which areas to discuss. Typical things that we the authors were able to ignore as parents were messy rooms, expressions of personal style (hair color, clothes, etc.), extracurricular activities, and homework. Things we felt were worth fighting over were church attendance, curfews, dishonesty, family obligations, and family chores.

Make a list of your priority battles. Who is affected by the particular behavior? Is the behavior worth fighting over (provided it isn't morally wrong or damaging to them or you)? When my (Boni's) daughter decided to make her own clothes (during her hippy stage) and wear a sewn-up tablecloth to school, I sure didn't like it. But it didn't impact the family directly. When she threw her clothes over the carpet in her room, we preferred that she hang them up, but that was her space. However, when she left her things in the common areas of the house, that did impact our family life. So this is what Don and I took issue with.

Think about how you would handle a confrontation with a friend. Most likely you would get together at an agreed-upon place, at a time that is convenient for both of you. You would also let this friend know something about what you want to discuss. Don't do any less for your children.

For example, my (Boni's) friend Janet told me about a confrontation with her daughter Natalie. She had reminded her normally responsible daughter to empty the dishwasher before she went to bed, but when Janet came home she saw that the dishwasher was still full. She stormed up the stairs to her sleeping daughter, flipped on the light, and demanded that Natalie do it now! When her daughter stumbled from bed, crying and sick with a migraine, Janet realized she had made a huge mistake. Don't be disrespectful when you discipline.

Speak respectfully and inquisitively to your preteens. Find out what they were thinking and why things happened as they did, and really pay attention to how they see the situation. Don't presume guilt or irresponsibility until you have heard the whole story. Ted gave his daugh-

Conflict Rules

- Pick a time and place that works for both of you
- Be respectful
- Ask questions and listen to the answers
- Stick to the subject
- Use natural and logical consequences in disciplining

ter Kaylie permission to go to the park with friends, providing she be home by 6:30. When he got a call from her at 7:00, he was furious and ready to confront her. But he stopped to hear Kaylie out before making a judgment. It turned out that the girls were approached by a man in the park and became frightened. They decided to stay together, not walking alone to their own homes. Going to the house of her friend meant that Kaylie was late. When Ted realized Kaylie was wise in her decision, he had a very different feeling about the situation. Ask questions that allow your children to explain what happened. You still may not hear what you hope to hear, but at least you have addressed the issue respectfully.

Common Conflicts and Consequences

Faith Issues

A father is distraught because his daughter has not made a commitment to Christ. He is angry and wants to put all sorts of limitations on her activities until she gets this area of her life right. Granted, this is a fearful area for parents. We long for our children to believe wholeheartedly in Jesus as their Savior and Lord. But we cannot make it happen. We can be sure they attend worship services regularly, but we cannot control their heart toward God. Since we cannot control it, we best not take responsibility for it beyond providing a safe place for them to grow into their faith.

Drugs and Alcohol

Some things cannot be tolerated because they have a lasting impact on our children. Anything that limits our children's choices later in life should be discussed with an attempt to change their behavior. Drugs and alcohol are in this category. We'll discuss this issue in more detail in the next chapter.

Homework

Hopefully you've gotten yourself out of the homework struggle by the time your child is a preteen. If not, you still have time. Remember, it is your child's homework, not yours. If you are the one with all the anxiety about whether homework gets done, you've taken responsibility for what you cannot control. But you can have some leverage. Make sure you have discussed with your child what your expectations are for homework. Let them know that just as the work you do to provide for your family is a priority, you expect that they will make their schoolwork a priority. You expect that they will take it seriously and do reasonably well at it. Then—and this is the hardest part—turn it over to them to manage. Offer to help only when they ask.

Logical consequences can be applicable here. Agree ahead of time on a consequence that is logical in nature. For example, you and your son may agree that should he get an F in a course, he will have to retake that course during the summer and pay for it himself. The advantage of setting up logical consequences ahead of time is that it keeps you out of a power struggle, eliminates unnecessary parental interference, and teaches children to take responsibility for their actions.

Chores

A common complaint we hear about in family therapy sessions involves family chores. The battle begins with parents hounding, preteens postponing; parents threatening, preteens doing the task badly; parents exploding and taking away privileges, and preteens rebelling even further. It becomes a vicious cycle that has parents more frustrated and exhausted than the preteens. So how can we as parents get preteens to participate in household tasks without setting off the stress alarm?

First, kids want to have some choice (what, when, how) in the matter. Your preteens may feel this even more than they did as children, because school activities often make it more difficult for them to find time for chores. When involved in extracurricular activities such as sports, they may need to change chore times around. For instance, it can be an added burden for them to be responsible for dinner cleanup when they get home late from soccer practice and still have homework to do. The weekend may be a more appropriate time to do chores. Make changes that work for them.

Chores

- Allow for chore choices (what, when, how to participate)
- Be flexible with schedules
- Don't nag or remind—use consequences
- State clearly what is expected and when it is to be completed
- Clearly define consequences for not completing agreed-upon chores

Also, clearly define what's expected. Does cleaning the bathroom include the floor and mirror, or just the sink, toilet, and tub? These things need to be spelled out. State when the chore is to be completed as well. Saying "These chores need to be finished by 5:00 Saturday afternoon" keeps you from nagging. Make sure everyone understands the consequences, and let them take their course.

Here are some ideas about consequences that are logically related to the undone chore. Let's say that Mom is having company on Sunday, and Joey has not done his vacuuming chore. So Mom does it on Saturday night and charges him a fee for maid service at the current rate of fifteen dollars per hour. Since it was his responsibility to get the chore done, Joey must foot the bill for her services. Allison's chore is to empty the dishwasher each morning. When it is not empty, dirty dishes are left in the sink. Now she has the added chore of rinsing off the dirty dishes and loading as well as emptying the dishwasher. If things get too messy and Mom can't cook dinner that night, pizza is ordered in at Allison's expense. She has just treated the family to dinner.

The family meeting can be used to discuss what must be done each week and who is in charge of that particular activity. This is a time to request changes about chores or consequences. For instance, Joey may ask for a note reminding him to vacuum, no matter how late it is on Saturday night. The family might agree to let him vacuum, even at midnight, knowing he prefers this to a dip in his allowance. If this solution works for everyone, the change can be made.

Complaints about cleanliness standards also may be an issue to discuss. Mandy thinks her dad's standards for cleaning the bathroom are unreasonable. Does she really have to clean the grout with a toothbrush every week? The family may then brainstorm together about more reasonable cleanliness standards. When dealing with your family, be flexible and listen to how they feel about chores. Of course, if the standard is so low that you can't tell if a chore has been accomplished, this is also a matter to discuss. When the entire family agrees on the standard, your

preteen knows she lets everyone down if she does a substandard cleaning job.

Eating Disorders

In a society that is driven by sex appeal, body image, and fitness, many
girls starve themselves in an effort to match their bodies to the ones they
see on models or in the movies. While boys also can develop this disorder, girls are most often affected by it. Eating as little as one hundred
calories a day, many anorexics allow themselves to become so weak that
medical attention is necessary. Some have hurt their bodies so severely
that life support is needed—and still they see themselves as too fat. In
the bulimic form of this disorder, enormous amounts of food are eaten
and then vomited immediately afterward. The number of times the
bulimic binges and purges increases after time, and many do this ten
times or more a day!

We can't give a comprehensive overview of eating disorders here, but
many books are available on the subject. We do want to stress the importance of parents taking this behavior seriously. Most often, eating disorders become worse; they rarely solve themselves. And they often
involve other issues such as control, self-esteem, body image, and peer
acceptance. If your child begins losing weight quickly, or if you notice
large amounts of food disappearing from your home, talk to her about
her eating patterns. If you suspect a problem, get help from a qualified
therapist. Eating disorders are progressive and are much easier to treat
early on rather than when they have become a fixed habit. Get help as
soon as you recognize the problem.

Parents Are Human Too!

Being a parent to a preteen can be emotionally agonizing and frustrating. Perhaps it is one of the most exhausting periods of parenthood.
There is so much activity going on, and everyone seems to need a ride
from you! Then there are the weekend nights with friends that seem to
last long after you would like to be in bed! Gone are the days when you
sent the kids to bed at 8:00 and had the evening to yourself. At this stage,
it is more often the case that you put *yourself* to bed and remind the kids
to turn out the lights!

Besides the exhaustion, there is little privacy for parents when children have similar sleep schedules to theirs. Spousal affection is much
easier before preteens enter the picture. You and your spouse will find

yourselves craving time alone as a couple but also find it harder to arrange now that your children are older. Going off together is not so easy. Preteens don't want a "baby-sitter," but they can't be left at home alone for long periods of time either. Everything becomes more complicated with these near-adults!

No matter how difficult it is, we encourage you to continue making your marriage a priority. One of the best gifts parents can give to preteens is a secure and loving marital relationship. Your children need to observe you making time for yourself individually and as a couple. And it will be only a few years before you and your spouse are alone again; hopefully you will not be strangers to each other when that happens.

We know of parents who take "time off" from their parenting duties. By letting their children know that when their door is closed, they are off duty (unless in case of an emergency or a serious issue or problem), the kids learn to respect their parents' need for quiet time. Other parents schedule a Saturday morning breakfast or a regular night out together each week. Parents need the refreshment that comes from being an adult without parental responsibilities. Explaining this to your preteen will make sense to them, and they can be enlisted in making sure you get the time you need.

So take time to be together without your children. Be affectionate with passing hugs and kisses. Sneak in times to cuddle and take time to laugh. If you are a single parent, stay connected with your support system. Find time away from your children that nourishes and refreshes you. Draw on extended family and community to help keep you sane! You will be a better parent for it.

Spiritual Implications

The way we present God to our children has a huge effect on how they view God and themselves in relationship to him. So look to the Holy Spirit to empower you to be Christlike in your interactions with your preteen. The Christian life is a natural progression from simple faith to a deep knowledge of God. As we face ourselves in many new ways as parents, the transforming process brings us into a deeper dependency on God's power.

Spiritually, many of us are in the "preteen" stage of development. We know what we are to be doing in our lives, yet we resist being mature in other areas. We know the areas of our lives that God objects to, yet we cry out "Why not!" in rebellion. We want to be in control of our lives, yet we know that we can do nothing without God's help. In spite of our rebellion, God patiently leads us. He never runs out of patience with his children as he continually prods, directs, provides, and encourages us to grow into spiritual maturity.

May God grant us the ability to follow Christ as we bring a stability into our children's lives that encourages and supports them through these tough preteen years.

Reflection Questions

1. Is there anyone who can meet with you on a regular basis to discuss your relationship with your preteen? Make a point to form a regular time to get together for support. Do you ever go "off duty"? Why or why not?
2. What are some ways you have dealt with the emerging sexuality of your child? How could you improve in this area? Think of two concrete things you can do.
3. How do you deal with anger? What helps you monitor your strong emotional reactions? Keep track how you do this week. Were you aware of what was behind the anger? How can you assist your preteen to deal better with his or her emotions?

8

Teenagers

Change and Transformation

When asked whether a teenager is a child or an adult, most people have a difficult time giving a precise answer. In terms of determining age of majority, different states have different ideas about when an adolescent has the right to marry without parental consent. In terms of voting privileges or military service, a person must be eighteen; for driving a car a person must be sixteen; but to attend most entertainment events, twelve is the age when a person must pay full admission price. The teenager is asked to pay adult prices, but when it comes to seeking adult privileges, they are told they have to wait to grow up. No wonder kids go crazy trying to figure out these "in between" years! In addition, after they get an education to help them qualify and compete for highly skilled jobs, they find that jobs are hard to find. Does this mean all adolescents experience an identity crisis? Of course not! But most teenagers experience some emotional turmoil on the way to becoming mature adults.

In some societies, there is no such thing as adolescence. There are two categories of people: children and adults. Children are treated like children, free from adult demands and excluded from making adult decisions. Adults are treated like adults, having both the rights and responsibilities that adulthood brings. Children make a successful passage from childhood to adulthood by going through initiation and puberty rites from which they emerge as full-fledged adults. Don't we wish it were so simple for our youth! Being a teenager in our society can be compared to being Alice in Wonderland. They grapple through a maze in a strange world of conflicting messages and rules.

The "generation gap" is real. We have a difficult time understanding the youth of each new generation, because we haven't lived through it in the way they have. Even the most "with it" parents can't keep up with the fast pace and changes in music and teen flicks that are popular with youth. Without a doubt, the adolescent subculture has a powerful influence. Wearing the right clothes, having the right hairstyle, playing the "in" music, speaking the right slang are the prescriptions for a "sweet," "excellent," "cool," "rad" (or whatever the right word is now) identity. Even youth who have a fairly solid identity in Christ will follow peer standards to be acceptable in external matters.

Developmental Tasks

So what do teenagers have in mind as they maneuver through the murky waters of adolescence? What are the tasks they have in common as they look to the future? There are three developmental tasks that will need to be accomplished as they move into adulthood.

Developing Autonomy

Developing autonomy has to do with teenagers taking responsibility in social, financial, and structural areas of life. While not totally independent, teens are beginning to establish meaningful relationships with peers and adults outside of as well as inside the family. In the financial area, though parents provide the basics (housing, food, and education), teenagers take on part-time or summer jobs to meet personal expenses, such as paying for gas, buying clothes, or going on dates. They also take care of their own personal needs like laundering clothes, arranging for transportation, nutrition, and sleep habits, etc.

Three Major Tasks for Teens to Accomplish

- Developing autonomy (taking more responsibility for self, identity in Christ)
- Developing interpersonal skills (gender interaction, tolerance, dating)
- Developing purpose (morality, career, life tasks, religious beliefs)

Developing Interpersonal Relationships

Developing interpersonal relationships is a high priority for young adults. They care deeply about their friends, and through the socializing process they learn to communicate and problem solve, develop significant emotional connections, show tolerance for different races, ages, and religions, and clarify their values in life choices and decisions.

Developing Purpose

Developing purpose is a task that includes work and career decisions, lifestyle choices, and moral and spiritual values. Teens realize there is meaning beyond the self, and they find ways to be an integral part of the larger society. Many are inclined to sacrifice themselves for a cause, go on a mission to build homes for the poor, or spend a year in another culture to expand their sense of purpose. Many also solidify their personal beliefs and commitments by examining, questioning, and sometimes challenging their parents' beliefs. Parents may be tempted to forcefully persuade rather than allow their teens to grapple honestly with doubts and questions at this point. But this is a mistake.

How well we (the Balswicks) remember the day Joel began expressing political views that were quite different from our own. At first, we found ourselves a little hurt that he hadn't swallowed our ideas hook, line, and sinker. In fact, Jack started to challenge Joel in a rather aggressive way, which only made Joel hold on more tenaciously to his ideas. Even though Jack could easily shoot holes in Joel's "half-baked" positions, it only caused Joel to fire back.

Fortunately, we realized this only made things worse. So we took a different tactic. The next time Joel tried out his new thoughts on us, we showed interest in how he was coming to his conclusions. Instead of being critical, we helped him think more deeply about the opinions that accompanied his point of view. We stopped trying to persuade him of our views and took time to understand how and why he was thinking the way he was. It was helpful to remind ourselves that when we were in college, we actually held to many of the same views he was espousing. We were simply at a different place at our time in life. When we had tolerance for Joel's views, it gave him freedom to ask questions and learn more about our ideas as well.

Young adults need to claim values and beliefs as their own, and patience is needed while they are finding their way. Answer questions honestly, giving reasons for your value system. Ask thoughtful questions and be genuinely interested in their ideas. This dialogue can be a wonderfully enriching time between parents and young adults.

Being self-directed, taking a responsible role in the family and community, and having the necessary skills to move toward a career goal are evidence of maturity. This is what we hope for our teens, but it's not always automatic or easy to get there.

Developing a Sufficient Self

The dramatic end of childhood dependence is the beginning of a search for independence. Young people are trying to find their own voice in the midst of many competitive voices of influence from family and society. Finding a sufficient self often brings inner turmoil as well as personal satisfaction. Frederich Buechner writes of his own experience in *The Sacred Journey* (1982, pp. 72–73):

> We search, on our journeys, for a self to be, for other selves to love, and for work to do.
> I can remember at least the sense of having become, or started to become, a self with boundaries somewhat wider than and different from those set by my family. I no more knew who I was then than in most ways I know who I am now, but I knew that I could survive more or less on my own in more or less the real world. I knew, as I had not before, the sound of my own voice both literally and figuratively—knew something of what was different about my way of speaking from anybody else's way and knew something of the power of words spoken from the truth of my own heart or from as close to that truth as I was able to come then.

Transition periods are times of uncertainty for parents and adolescents alike. We as parents feel a bit uneasy because we may not be prepared to handle our teenagers' push for becoming their own person. It is indeed a process we live through. We (the Balswicks) remember how confident Jacque was at sixteen years old when she got her driver's license. One evening when she was going out the door to drive to a friend's house, Judy called out to her to be careful because it was raining. Jacque gave her a look of disdain and replied in a rather indignant tone of voice, "Oh, Mom! I can handle it!" However, less than fifteen minutes later we received a phone call and heard the frightened voice of a child on the other end of the line. "Mommy, I just got in an accident. Can you come? I don't know what to do!" A totally independent teenager one moment became a distraught little girl the next. Back and forth it goes, on the way to becoming an independent adult.

A young person must be sufficiently connected to have the strength to be separate, just as having a separate self allows them to make the deepest connection with others. However, in some homes the connection is so binding that it's difficult for the adolescents to establish a separate identity. The family is like permanent glue in which family members are stuck together. Each member's sense of self is tightly bound up with the parents, making it difficult to form a self who has separate thoughts. Out of frustration, youth in these homes may rebel as a way to break free of the stuck-togetherness.

At this point in our kids' lives, we can do nothing other than entrust them to God's care. We need to let them establish lives and selves that reflects their ideas and values. We need to encourage them by helping them see their worth and value. We need to affirm a purpose and meaning through faith in God. We need to point to the power of the Holy Spirit to enable them to live their lives for Christ. We need to empower them through our prayers, support, and continual love. And finally, we must relinquish them to the Lord.

Developing a Sexual Self

Teens want to know the truth about sex! And they want parents to affirm sex rather than just give the caution and danger talks. So give them clear, accurate information they can trust and verify that sex was God's idea. You can let them know that sex is intended for a deeply satisfying, person-centered union between spouses.

Discuss the implications of a secular value system that leads to nonrelational sex. In fact, the current term "hooking up" is a graphic depiction of nonrelational sex norms! Two people hook up body parts for a few moments of pleasure, with no real emotional attachment to each other. It is important for kids to know that nonrelational sexual morality is contrary to God's relation-centered covenant commitment.

You should affirm celibacy as a gift one wholeheartedly brings to the marriage union. Applaud your teens when they stand firm for celibacy. Let them know that it takes courage and conviction to say "no" to peer pressure and media falsehoods about sex. After all, it's difficult to counter the popular trend that puts sex on a pedestal, promising much more that it can deliver. It takes a sufficient self to live according to a consistent moral value system.

Dialogue about the issues rather than give a lesson in morality whenever the topic comes up. A study by Walters and Walters (1980) indicated that open discussion of sexuality in the home (the more discussions the better) was related to postponement of sexual activity and to responsible use of contraceptives in youth. Hopefully, you'll be able to discuss the pros and cons of contraception, abortion, AIDS, and the morality behind sexual decisions. You should be clear that the only 100 percent safe sex is not to have sex before marriage. In other words, there is no safe way to break God's commandment.

There are many reasons why teenagers engage in sexual intercourse. Perhaps one reason is because it is an area that parents really cannot

Positive Things Parents Can Do to Promote Godly Sexual Attitudes

- Be a good model of relationship-focused love
- Present sex as God's good gift for marriage
- Uphold the value of celibacy
- Discuss implications of steady dating/exclusive relationships
- Affirm friendship and group dating
- Teach teens how to say "No!" to unwanted sexual behavior
- Stay connected with your teenagers and their friends

control. And if your teenager chooses to be sexually active, the best thing you can do is keep the discussion open. Show compassion should they make a mistake, and assure them that God's grace and forgiveness wipes the slate clean so they can start over again. Virginity is a matter of the heart and mind as well as the body.

Permeable Boundaries

A boundary can be thought of as an imaginary line that defines personal territory, both physical and emotional. If we intrude on boundaries carelessly, we will undoubtedly be greeted with an all-out barricade of defense. Regard for physical boundaries means not intruding where we don't belong. Resist overstepping the line.

Boundaries having to do with emotional comfort zones may be a bit more challenging and subtle. How do you respond when your daughter wears something you think looks awful, or when your son does something weird to his hair? This takes extra care and thought. If we attempt to determine how our teenagers should dress or wear their hair, we demonstrate a lack of consideration for their preferences, ideas, and feelings.

Adolescence is a time to negotiate distance and closeness in relationships. Sometimes a teenager will erect thick walls peppered with warning signs such as "Do Not Enter." Especially during the crucial time when teens are trying to establish independence, they are extremely vigilant when parents cross boundaries recklessly. It easily can become a friction zone, so you must approach any boundary with proper credibility and care. The following example illustrates this point.

Derek and his friend were having a friendly conversation in the family room. Unannounced, Derek's mother, Mary, walked into the room, interrupted the conversation, and offered her strong opinions about the topic. While the boys politely tolerated the intrusion, it dampened their spirited discussion. They immediately remembered they had to meet some friends at the local pizza parlor. Derek dismissed himself to change into his jeans, while Mary continued talking to the friend, telling him all about Derek's childhood. Suddenly, she remembered a great picture of Derek as a nude baby, and she proceeded to knock on Derek's bedroom door to get it. Hearing her knock, he asked her to wait because he was dressing. Mary disregarded his request and barged into his room, saying, "Oh, don't be silly! I'm just coming in to get your picture. I won't look at you anyway!"

Need we say anything further? This mother not only violated the emotional and physical boundaries of her son, but she also was totally unaware of the disrespectful intrusion. This situation was more than a skirmish; it was a battle that will probably keep Derek away from home as much as possible. This lack of self-awareness on Mary's part led to a serious breach of boundary.

Remember that well-defined boundaries are building blocks that help you develop respectful and accountable ways to live with teenagers.

Discipline Empowerment

Who is in the driver's seat now that your teenager is old enough to drive? In most instances, teens want nothing more than to get behind the wheel—to gain more control over their lives and determine where they're going. But parents may hesitate to give up the wheel because they fear their teenagers will make wrong turns in life.

Overly restrictive parents hold on too tightly to the wheel, constraining independence. Rigid rule setting gives teenagers no "breathing space" to think and act out of their own convictions. While they may be obliged to obey now, they may rebel later on when parents aren't around to enforce the rules. More subtle reactions to overly strict control are physical rebellions such as bulimia or anorexia. These actions are a way of saying, "I'm in control and you can't control what I put in my mouth or what I choose to vomit!" It's a drastic way to rebel since it can lead to bodily harm and even death. Family therapy is an avenue to help in such situations.

Permissive parenting is also confusing when teens are trying to establish independence. Overly permissive parents are reluctant to define the rules, allowing teens to decide on their own. Don't be fooled. Teenagers need parameters, because without clearly stated rules or limits, they must discover limitations through trial and error. The ambiguity may take them to extreme behaviors in their search for norms. Teenagers need parental guidance, and when you fail to take sufficient leadership, they interpret this as a lack of interest in them.

Things get even more confusing when Mom and Dad polarize into overly strict and overly permissive roles. It's a "good parent/bad parent" competition that pulls parents apart. Parents who operate together with moderate disciplinary practices do best when dealing with adolescents. It takes a good balance of parental power in order for families to be effective. There is evidence that parental happiness, positive child-rearing practices, and united authority between Mom and Dad are predictive of fewer instances of adolescent rebellion.

Discipline is a matter of keeping balance, being adaptable, working together as parents, and using the delegating modality. While we concede it's difficult to stop being a child, it's also difficult to stop being a parent! In fact, trusting teenagers to make the right choices and act responsibly may be one of the hardest things a parent is called upon to do. It's risky for two reasons: (1) This is a true test of the teenager's ability to act responsibly, and (2) this is a true test of the parents' success in empowering them to be responsible.

I (Don) remember an argument with my father when I was seventeen. He and I often argued, and had since I was thirteen. This time the argument was over whether or not I could go out late on a Saturday night. We were both angry. Finally, nose-to-nose with me, he said, "You will not go!" I looked him in the eye and said, "I'm going. How will you stop me?" Suddenly I could see in his eyes that he knew he couldn't stop me. I was bigger and stronger than he was. Realizing that scared me. It made me stop and think. I realized that whether I obeyed him or not depended on me, not him. From that time on I considered what he said to me with more thought than I had ever given before. I also tended to be more obedient and easier to get along with than I had been at thirteen, fourteen, fifteen, and sixteen.

It does no good to force teenagers to be obedient. Parents need to bring their children to the place where they respect adults enough to consider what they have to say and make decisions on respect rather than fear or rebellion. And parents need to respect their teenagers' ability to make good choices.

How to Do Battle?

We have mentioned the importance of discerning carefully which battles to fight and which to ignore. Yet parents shouldn't ignore a real problem, hoping it will eventually go away. It may be that our children intend to act contrary to God's will. Their behavior may not affect them developmentally but instead may have an enormous impact on their commitment to Christ or their desire to be part of a community of believers.

When we think of the battles that are waged in war, we think of blood, injury, and death. That is exactly what we don't want to happen in our relationships with our children. Our goal must always be to encourage them toward God and thus toward personal growth. Pouts, screams, fights, manipulation, and permanent damage through words or actions are not the answer. Screaming, "I found drugs in your pocket! You're grounded!" or "I am going to force this food down your throat and you will never purge again. Do you hear me, young lady!" are not ways of talking to someone we respect or hope to encourage.

Empowerment always has the purpose of showing love, demonstrating respect, and creating a dialogue to bring about change. Ultimately, it is the decision of the teen to change his or her behavior. All we can do is hope for a discussion and an exchange that is thought provoking for everyone. Hopefully, as we talk with our kids, we will come to know each other more fully. Making ourselves available in this interchange is the most important thing we can do.

If we treat our teenagers as we would a friend whom we dearly love and are deeply concerned about, we will find a way of talking with them that is respectful as well as shows our love and concern for them.

Common Conflicts and Consequences

There are several issues that come up again and again between parents and teens. Issues of homework, chores, anger, eating disorders, and mood swings defined in the previous chapter will continue to need attention in the teen years. Parents will need to continue to work together with kids to negotiate these areas of potential conflict. Let's discuss a few other possible problem areas.

Driving

Most teens are eager to drive, and most parents are conflicted about them doing so. On the one hand, it may mean less carpooling for us; on the other hand, it puts great fear into our hearts. We'll need to navigate these frightening waters together.

Driving is usually under our control. Until teenagers leave the home, we decide who gets the keys and when. Most teens drive the family car and come under the family insurance plan. This gives us leverage! While we may understand the potential disasters that can occur because of irresponsible driving, teens rarely believe that anything bad will happen to them. Thus we the parents set the standards for driving.

Many parents set fairly strict guidelines with children during the first months in which they have their license. Not having friends in the car for the first six months, only driving to school functions, not driving after midnight, never having more than four friends in the car at a time are ways parents can attempt to make driving a safe and gradual privilege. Most parents prohibit driving if drugs or alcohol become a part of the teenagers' lives.

Often auto insurance companies give a percentage break to students with B averages, because these students have fewer accidents. Therefore, if you're paying the insurance, the "good student" benefit keeps the fee lower. Then it should be the responsibility of your teenager to pay the extra expense when the B average is not maintained.

Driving is not a privilege if the parents rescue the kids each time they mess up. Natural consequences work well with driving. When your daughter is caught speeding, she should be obligated either to pay the speeding ticket or lose her driver's license. Don't bail her out, but instead expect her to comply with the law. And if your son scratches the car, he should be the one to get it fixed.

Drugs

"What if my kid is on drugs!" The fears in this area, especially if we believe the statistics that say the majority of kids do drugs before they reach eighteen, either put us in extreme denial or extreme anxiety! Many teens are recreational drug users who do not see the dangers involved. Actually, most of them think of drug use as a normal part of adolescence. The thought of permanent damage, addiction, car accidents, or lax sexual behaviors that may end in pregnancy rarely occurs to teens. What then are we to do?

The best defense against drugs is a good relationship with you. Openly discuss the issues with them. Know your drugs; be informed about what is available in your area and what the trends are. Know the lingo. Rarely will a teen say, "I am going to go do drugs tonight." Rather, they talk about smack and bowls. Be alert to what the words mean. Talk with your teen about what they are tempted by and why. Ask questions like, "What is the draw for you?" "How can I help?" "How available is it?" Ask these things in the most matter-of-fact way you can muster, because harsh lectures and reactivity will shut down your teen.

Many parents set up a "no consequence" contract in which they promise to come get their teens if they call any time they are in a vulnerable situation or are under the influence. The plan is for the parents to come immediately, regardless of the time, without any threat of punishment. The message is clear: "We care about you and your safety above all else." At a later time, a calm discussion can be had to process what happened and what needs to be done to avoid a similar situation in the future.

If you find drugs in your home or know that your child is drinking or using, do not hesitate to bring up your concerns. Use the respectful approach that we have discussed throughout this book and give your child an opportunity to explain. Don't be so reactive that the conversation ends before it begins. And also keep in mind that teens can be deceitful in ways that leave parents clueless. So don't be stupid! Parents who put on the blinders of denial are easily deceived. Even when evidence is right before their eyes, they choose not to believe what they see.

My (Boni's) friend Sally told me a few years ago about a young teen in her youth group that was brought to her house completely drunk. Ali's friends were fearful of taking her home, but they also were scared about her condition. Sally stayed with her through the night as she vomited, cried, and was completely disoriented. The next day when they talked, Sally realized that Ali had a real problem. She told Ali that she would be calling her parents and that she hoped Ali would talk to them before she did. Ali agreed and left for home.

A few hours later, Sally called Ali's parents to explain the situation. Ali's mother wouldn't believe Sally until she talked to her daughter about it. Sally was disappointed that Ali had not kept her promise to tell her parents, and she was even more disappointed when Ali's mom called back. She was hostile and accused Sally of lying about her daughter. "I believe my daughter when she says she only had one beer and that you are exaggerating!" How unfortunate that this mother couldn't open her eyes and confront Ali at the time. Now, years later, Ali has a serious drug problem that won't go away with wishes.

Remember that drug use starts at younger ages these days. Educate yourself, know the signs, and look for them. Don't let things go. Ask when you don't understand. Take it on as your problem by saying, "Hey, you know I'm scared to death about stuff like this, so just let me ask some things, okay? Why did you seem disoriented last night? Why does your friend slur his words? Help me understand what is going on here because I can be a little thick." If you find trouble, take it seriously. Get your teen the help they need. Keep your head out of the sand and stay on top of the drug temptation that every teen faces.

Dating

The questions for parents are usually, "When should teens be allowed to date? Or should they even be dating at all?" While it's good to talk to your teenager about the purpose of dating and why he or she wants to participate, dating is often a matter where parents differ.

We (the Pipers) remember the many discussions we had with our daughter Sarah before she could go out on a date. We would ask all the usual questions our parents asked us. "Where are you going?" "When do you expect to be home?" "Who will be there?" One question was different, however. "Which one of you is driving?" That was a question that was never asked when we were young. Boys always did the driving. That's not the case anymore. Nor do boys always do the calling or arranging. Kids today look at dating differently than those of past generations.

When should couples be allowed in a car alone? Do parents need to know the people their teens are with? If so, how well do they need to know them? These issues can be a source of conflict for parents. Just ask us (the Pipers). Don, who had gotten into a fair amount of trouble as a teen, had fears about his daughters going out on dates. In his desire to protect them, he set different rules with them than he had with his son. Of course, this did not seem fair to the girls, and I (Boni) tended to agree. A lot of talking had to take place for Don and me to agree on how to deal with this dating discrepancy.

The girls still did not like the fact that their dad had to meet any guy they were going to go out with. But once they understood that his concern was for their safety (Don wanted the boys to have personal knowledge that the girls had a father who cared about them), and once they had the opportunity to express how stupid they thought it was, and once they found out the guys didn't really mind that much, it was okay. (At least Don wasn't as extreme as one friend of mine, who says to his daughter, "You need to invite the boys home so I can show them my guns!") The important thing was for Don and me to come together with a plan we could agree on.

The most important principles here are those of love and respect among parents and teens. We are people of God who want to give good things to our children, as God gives so many good things to us. And as parents who love and long to protect our children in healthy ways, we shouldn't give to our teens what they cannot handle. So we should know our teens! Since the hormones are raging, it's best they not be freely unleashed! Instead, they need limits. So talk about what they want and what the parameters will be.

Many compromises are possible. A specific age to begin dating is usually sixteen. Before that time, you may negotiate mixed-gender group events or permit school-sponsored dating events or allow your teen to get used to being around the opposite sex through church youth-group events. Stick to what you have decided and what you believe is right for your teen, while still listening to his or her feelings. Be flexible and accommodate when it's reasonable.

I (Boni) recall an incident when my family was living in Northern Ireland for a year. Karlie was fifteen years old and had not begun dating. Near the end of our stay there, she asked us if she could go walking around the neighboring town with a boy from school. The plan was to meet the boy after school, take the train to a town a few miles away, walk around, get something to eat, and then be picked up by us. This sounded like a date to Don and me. "No, this is just hanging out," Karlie insisted. But this "hanging out" seemed very important to her. We knew she really liked this boy and was excited about seeing the town and hanging out like the rest of her peers. After much discussion, we decided to let her do this, but, true to form, Don wanted to meet the boy. Karlie pleaded, "No! Don't make it bigger than it is! How embarrassing!" Of course, Don imagined some big guy with a shaved head and jackboots taking his daughter off on a train ride (five miles!) to who knows where! No way was his daughter getting on a train with a guy he didn't even know! The longer he thought about it, the bigger the guy became in his mind.

Finally an agreement was reached. Don drove into town to meet Karlie after school. She came to the car with her friend and introduced a frightened, skinny, short boy to Don, who shook his hand and said, "Have a good time. I'll be back here at 7:00." Don's fears evaporated as he realized the boy was in fact a boy. And everyone lived through it.

As a result of that experience, Don and I learned the value of having clear rules. We also learned to trust our daughter and be flexible when that was called for. And it set a precedent for how things would go in the future.

Parents Are Human Too!

A unique problem at this life stage is that while teenagers are on a quest for independence, parents are entering midlife. Although not all parents experience midlife as a crisis (some even will be entering their most creative years), most of us will be reevaluating our lives during this stage. Whether you're wondering about the lofty goals you have not achieved or are reluctantly accepting what is, you're on somewhat of a downhill trajectory. Some of you may be bored with the routines of life, wishing for something more exciting, while others may be tired of trying to keep a competitive edge. You may compare yourself with others and think you've not achieved as much as they have.

Mothers who entered the workforce after childbearing years may find there is no realistic way to "catch up" for lost time in experience or training. And those who have dedicated their lives to parenthood find that teens want less of them and will soon be gone. These mothers may be haunted by the questions "What next? What can I do in the outside world?" And in general, parents may be asking themselves, "Is this all there is? What have I given my life for?"

At this stage, we're also keenly aware of same-age friends who are dying of heart attacks and cancer, and our own health issues become a concern. Fathers compare their aging bodies with teenage muscle mass. While your adolescent boy finds his muscles enlarging and physical strength increasing, you may find your muscles shrinking and your strength declining. You may even start jogging or lifting weights to overcome the discrepancy. And while mothers are fighting to keep their figures intact, teenage girls are beginning to develop firm figures. Your daughter is in the prime of her physical beauty, while you are working hard to maintain what you have. As you walk down the street with your adolescent daughter, you may come to realize the whistles are for her.

And then there are the parents who reach midlife after having worked long, hard hours at their jobs, only to realize their children are nearly grown. Saddened by the fact that they have spent little time and have had little impact on the lives of their children, they may want to establish the relationship at this late date. But now that they have time, their children are no longer interested.

Since these factors lead to internal and relational stress in the home, the teen years are likely to be a stormy time for both kids and parents. Balancing what is happening in our lives along with the trials in our adolescents' lives can be a harrowing challenge. Our task is to separate our internal struggles from the struggles of parenting our teens. Then we should find ways to take care of ourselves. Perhaps we may think of becoming part of a small support group of men or women where we can talk about our internal and relational struggles. Finally, we should be honest with our teenagers about some of the things we're facing and how we see it interfering with our relationships. During the vulnerability of this discussion, our teenagers have a chance to understand us better.

Spiritual Implications

To love children is easy when they freely give their love in return. To continue to love teenagers when they resist or reject our love is another matter. Whereas unconditional love is God's ideal, to love conditionally is a human tendency. But while there is nothing abnormal about the urge to withhold love when it's rejected, there is another option. Go the second mile.

Sometimes we feel the guilt of our failure as parents when our teens turn away. It brings out self-doubt about where we went wrong or what we could have done differently. And, for a variety of reasons, we may not have been all we could have been as parents. If we had it to do over again, all of us could think of ways in which we could relate differently to our children.

But most of us do the best we can under the circumstances. So we can take comfort in Hosea 11, in which God does not blame himself when the children of Israel go astray. Rather, he says he did all the right things. And we would agree that God did do the right things. He loved unconditionally, set limits, and gave wise guidance. Yet even this was no guarantee. Israel rebelled in spite of all that God did.

God declares, "I will not carry out my fierce anger, nor will I turn and devastate Ephraim. For I am God, and not man—the Holy One among you. I will not come in wrath" (Hosea 11:9 NIV). So in spite of rebellion, there is a way back. Christian parents must never, never close the door. There is no guarantee that our children will come back, but with God as our model and the Holy Spirit as our strength, we can hold out a hand of hope and pray they will return. And we can go the second or even the third mile whenever necessary.

Our hope is that our teenagers will have an identity that is centered in Christ, be responsible human beings, have formed interdependent relationships, and be enthusiastic about meaningful life goals. Research continues to show that religious beliefs and church attendance is a major factor that contributes to the emotional health of adolescents. We should want nothing less for our children. So hope and pray that their personal beliefs and value systems inform their lives with a sense of purpose and satisfaction. While they undoubtedly will make plenty of mistakes along the way, we long for them to arrive at mature adulthood. And when this happens, we can only thank the Lord.

Reflection Questions

1. What are some struggles you have faced with your teenager? Were they similar or dissimilar to your own teenage struggles? Explain. What specific things can you do to strengthen your relationship with your teenager?

2. Evaluate your family in regard to personal boundaries. Are you respectful of boundaries for all members of the family? Are there areas where this is hard for you? Why?
3. What has your midlife transition been like? Is it different for you as father or mother? What has helped you through it? How has God been present?

9

Leaving Home and Letting Go

How well we (the Pipers) remember the pain we felt the year we left our oldest child at college, three thousand miles away, and began the long drive home without him. We said little the first five hundred miles as our two daughters chattered in the backseat, trying to cheer us up and restore the joy to our vacation trip across the country. We were glad for their efforts, but nothing could take away the pain of not having him with us. So on we drove, sightseeing, picnicking, swimming, and laughing, all with an underlying sense of loss.

Later, in explaining this pain to a friend, we were asked if we had not wanted Aaron to go to college. Or was it the school he chose that upset us so much? Or were we fearful that something would happen to him? No, no, no, we said again and again. We just hadn't realized it would hurt so much! Our friend never quite understood what was wrong with us or why we had reacted the way we did to such a good thing happening to our family.

Two years later, after making the trip to drop our son *and* eldest daughter off at the same school, the ache was there again. Only this time two of our kids were gone! Stopping at another friend's home on the way back to Seattle, we talked again of the loss and the pain of missing them. "It's awful, isn't it?" our friend said knowingly. "Somebody should have told us about this time in a parent's life." We felt blessed to hear someone echo our feelings!

In all of our anguish, we often had another thought that amused us. What if they didn't go? That would be a different kind of anguish indeed! But somehow we just wanted it all to stay the same. For our children to be children forever. For us to be a family forever.

It's a good thing that God doesn't take all our thoughts and fears too seriously and give us what we think we want. Having gone through the leaving process with all our children, we are immensely enjoying relating to adult children who have their own ideas and goals for life. We hope that they continue to "orbit" at a safe distance from the family while still keeping a vital connection. How glad we are to see their independence, to hear of their dreams and adventures, and to see them used in God's kingdom. The joy we feel now is at least as great as the pain we had felt earlier.

The Leaving Process

This is the time of family life in which your high school graduates leave home to venture into life without you. The leaving-home day is a momentous event that marks a new beginning as well as an ending of life as it has been. It takes into account the past that is already known, the present that is full of ambiguity, and the future that holds the secret to what will be. This is a significant rite of passage that opens up sad and glad emotions in both parents and children. Whether the good-bye is a simple handshake, a wink and a smile, a shed tear, a prolonged hug, or an angry statement, it is a gesture that symbolizes the end and a beginning.

There are many ways to leave home. Some youth can't quite muster up the energy to take off, while others go such a distance that there is no longer a gravitating force to keep them connected to the family. As you can imagine, some leave-takings are better than others, but most get the job done. Herbert Anderson and Kenneth Mitchell have described a number of ways to leave in their book *Leaving Home* (1983).

1. *Leaving without it being noticed.* In this leaving, there is no acknowledgment of the leaving process. A child just moves out, and no one marks the move as significant. It could be thought of as a silent leaving, in that no one notices or pays attention.

Carla's leaving was like that. In high school, she began spending more and more time with her friends and less time with her single mom. When she was sixteen years old, she moved in with her boyfriend. She remembers no conversation with her mother regarding the move. There was no acknowledgment of the effect of this on their relationship or on Carla's life. She wasn't sure if her mom even cared that she was gone.

2. *The hidden departure.* This leaving happens without the parents' knowledge, as in the case of elopement or joining the military without informing anyone about the decision. It is a sneaky kind of leaving since the family is informed after the fact. Garrison Keillor (1994) tells about the hidden departure of Dale, a graduate of Lake Wobegone High School,

class of 1986. The day after graduation, Dale announced to his mother that he had joined the navy.

> "Why so soon?" his mother said. "Honey. You didn't. Oh Dale. How could you do this? Honey, you don't even know how to swim. You'd be out in the ocean some place."
>> "Ma, they carry life preservers."
>> "How do you know that?"
>> "It's the law, they have to."
>> "Who's going to enforce it?" (p. 71)

3. *The angry leaving.* Blaming can play a big role in this leaving experience. Sometimes the child blames the parents for his or her unhappiness ("You people drive me crazy!"), and sometimes the parents blame their child for disrupting the family ("You're impossible to live with!"). This leaving usually takes place after much conflict between the parents and young adult. Unable to resolve their differences, they escalate the fighting, and separation appears to be the only way out.

Natalie left her home in quite a huff! There was so much disruption that she felt the only thing to do was get out of her tumultuous household. Both she and her parents blamed each other for the abrupt departure.

4. *The pretended leaving.* This leaving is a ploy, because the parents are still in the driver's seat. Even though the adult child physically leaves home, he or she is still treated like a child and remains emotionally dependent on the parents. It may look like leaving on the outside, but no real changes have been made in the relationship.

Gary was the last of four children. When he moved into his own apartment, it seemed like the natural thing to do. His parents were excited for him, and his mother had lots of ideas on how to fix up his place. She brought him items for his kitchen, cooked him meals for his freezer, and even sneaked in to clean the place every now and then. His father called friends to check on how Gary was doing at work and tried to find out how Gary was handling his money. And Gary counted on their interventions. He knew his parents were always there to fall back on. But his leaving was a pretense. His parents' unhelpful holding on kept him from moving on.

5. *The unaccepted leaving.* In this case, the parents don't accept the fact that their adult child is really leaving home. They disregard their child's adult status, responding as if there were no change in the relationship. They make it clear from the time of departure that the leaving is unacceptable to them.

In the book *Godric* from a chapter entitled "How Godric Left Home," Frederick Buechner (1980) describes the leaving-home day of this twelfth-century holy man.

> "Farewell, Father. Mother, farewell," I said. Aedwen [mother] took and slowly turned my face from side to side as if to rummage it for something there she'd lost or feared to lose. She gave me a sack of berries and a wool cap. She wept no tears, and not a word came from her lips.
>
> Aedlward, my father, was sitting by the fire. He did not rise. He only raised one hand, then spoke the only word of all the words he ever spoke to me that I remember still as his.
>
> "You'll have your way, Godric," he said, and to this day that word he spoke and that raised hand are stitched together in my mind.
>
> I believe my way went from that hand as a path goes from a door, and though many a mile that way has led me since, with many a turn and cross-road in between, if ever I should trace it back, it's to my father's hand that it would lead. I kissed him on his head then, for he'd turned away to watch the flames. He smelled of oxen and of rain. It was the last I ever saw of him. When a man leaves home, some scrap of his heart waits there against his coming back. (p. 50)

6. *Matter-of-fact leaving.* In this leaving, there is a simple announcement and a clear acceptance of the new arrangement. Mixed feelings are openly acknowledged and dealt with. This intentional choice implies that adult children have developed enough sense of self to know what they want, and the parents celebrate this decision.

Kelsey had been planning to move into an apartment for more than a year. When she and her girlfriend finally had saved enough money to furnish and decorate the place and manage the first month's rent, Kelsey's parents were pleased to help with the move and celebrate her leaving with their best wishes.

The Fight for Separation

Have you ever noticed how often we bicker just prior to leaving those we love? It is almost as if the fighting helps us let go. A friend recalled how frustrating the summer had been before her son left for a year's trip to Europe. She and her husband rarely had difficulty with Jake while he was in high school, yet now that he was preparing to leave home, every discussion seemed to end in an argument. When his departure drew near, she was counting the days with eager anticipation! The whole family was ready, not out of a sense of hope for him and his future but out of exhaustion with the last months of disruption. While their family had seemed to be a close one, true feelings were rarely expressed. Since talking about how they felt did not seem like an option, Jake pushed the family away by being difficult. Jake acted out his fears, and the conflict was enough of a distraction to help him leave.

In this case, the family missed an opportunity. How much better it would have been if the parents and their son could have talked about what was going on inside each of them. Of course he was fearful of what was ahead, but he wanted to go anyway. Of course they would miss him a lot, but they also wanted him to succeed. What was communicated instead was turmoil and guilt.

Generally speaking, some form of emotional separation will happen during the leaving-home time. If we do not give our children permission to leave, to explore life with our blessing, most simply will leave without our blessing. They may do it with angry words. They may do it with tears and turmoil. Or they may do it by withdrawing emotionally. And the loss is not only theirs but ours as well. While they will miss out on our blessing and assurance of hope, we will miss out on the blessing of ongoing relationship with them. In their wonderful book *The Blessing* (1986), Gary Smalley and John Trent note how Isaac blessed his son Jacob by giving him a meaningful touch, a spoken message, a special affirmation, words of high value, and an active commitment. What a significant event it is, to be blessed with this kind of love.

Launching Losses

Regardless of how easy or difficult it is for young adults to leave home, loss is a significant part of the experience. The emotional and physical bonds will never be quite the same again. Family members must reorganize themselves to make up for the missing member. As the family shifts to accommodate the gaps, changes reverberate throughout the entire family system. Parents and adult children need to attend to the losses, feelings of fragmentation, isolation, and being out of sorts with one another.

Just as leaving home can be an ordeal between parents and their adult children, it is also an ordeal for brothers and sisters. It can be very painful, indeed, for the sibling(s) who is left behind. Regardless of whether the leave-taking is viewed as a celebration or a rejection, it always disrupts the status quo of sibling relationships. Unresolved conflicted relationships may be a source of guilt, or guilt may come from extra privileges and the achievement of a new place of importance after the older siblings are gone. In other situations, the leaving of older siblings gives the youngest children an opportunity to establish a different relationship with their parents. They finally get all the attention.

This seemed true of Sarah, the youngest of our (the Pipers') children. While she loved her older brother and sister deeply, she often had to work hard to get in her ideas and topics of discussion at the dinner table. And she'd had a lifetime of sharing our attention at sporting events and other activities she participated in. But when her older siblings left home, she finally had center stage and seemed to delight in it. Now we attended all her basketball games because we no longer had to divide our time between siblings. Dinnertime conversation seemed to center on her interests, and eventually she even got the bigger bedroom! Though she missed her brother and sister, she enjoyed the special attention she received during this period of life.

In other cases, a sibling's leaving is not only a blessing but also a burden. Catherine, the baby of the family, had many advantages after her older siblings left. She now had a beautifully decorated bedroom and a TV all to herself. Yet she felt incredibly lonely and lost without her siblings. The availability of her parents didn't make up for the missed company. While her parents now could attend all her school events, she missed having her brother and sister there to cheer her on. While she could invite friends over without having to worry about anyone else competing for space, home was a less exciting place without the presence of her siblings. And while she and her parents went out to eat at nicer restaurants, she was the single focus of attention when things went wrong. She had no one else to bounce off her ideas or negative feelings on when her parents seemed unreasonable. Since dinnertime had always been action-packed with talk, laughter, and differences of opinions, she now felt strange about the silence during the meal. She also had to pick up the slack by doing additional chores and felt more responsible for intervening between her parents when they argued.

Sibling birth order can be a troublesome factor in the leaving-home experience. When my (Judy's) older sister got married right out of high school and moved across the country to join her husband, who was enlisted in the navy, I was given opportunities to achieve in ways that had not been available to me before. I took full advantage and made plans to go to college. Later on, I felt guilty that my sister's choice to marry and have children at an early age had made it possible for me to receive additional financial support from my parents. As a middle child who sometimes played second fiddle, I had been promoted to the privileged first chair in the orchestra! The fact that I gained so much after she had left was something I had to reconcile with later on in life. I also had to deal with my frustration at being cheated out of seeing my younger brother's basketball success the year after I left home. We had been close friends all through high school, and it was a great loss for me when I wasn't able to attend his final state championship game.

Planning a Leaving-Home Ritual

- Set apart a time and day to have a family ceremony of leaving
- Use meaningful symbols to represent the relationship
- Express your appreciation for and what you will miss about the one who is leaving
- Have the one who is leaving express what the leaving means to him or her
- Include a burial of past hurts or disappointments, if this is appropriate

Oh yes! There is sadness in saying good-bye to those who leave. And there often is as much pain in leaving as there is in being left behind. So let's acknowledge the losses by finding a time and place to express what we feel so we can make peace with the leaving.

A Ritual of Leaving

Graduation day is a good example of a ritual that signifies a rite of passage into adulthood. A day is set apart for the graduation ceremony. Invitations are sent to family and friends so they can join the celebration with best wishes, cards, and presents to honor the graduate and his or her accomplishments on this special day.

Private leaving-home rituals can provide a similar opportunity to say good-bye. The purpose of a leaving-home ritual is to mark this event in a meaningful way. Here is an example of how the Pederson family made use of a good-bye ritual when Tim left home. Tim and his family had been at odds for about two years before he finally left home to take a job in another state. As a matter of fact, everyone was quite relieved when Tim finally announced his plans to leave home. Their family therapist asked each family member to bring an object (symbol) to the final therapy session to mark this transition in the life of the family.

There was a sense of anticipation and a little anxiety when they gathered together for this final session. Mr. Pederson started things off by pulling out his pocketknife. He and Tim had used this knife many times during their Boy Scout father-and-son camp-outs. Although the past years had been a struggle, Mr. Pederson wanted Tim to remember the many good times they'd had together as father and son. Mrs. Pederson brought a letter that she had written for the occasion. She read her thoughts out loud about freedom and forgiveness. Admitting her resentful feelings about a particular incident that had occurred in the past, she asked forgiveness for her judgmental attitude. Tim was able to receive her apology, lifting a long-felt burden between them. His sister gave Tim a little trinket mouse he had won for her at a county fair some years ago. She told him how much it meant to her to have a big brother who'd protected her when she'd felt as small as that little mouse. Tim's younger brother had drawn a picture of the two of them riding bikes together with a note saying how much he would miss him.

Next it was Tim's turn. Everyone was eager to know what he would do. With a grin on his face, he revealed the key to his bedroom door. He had used this key to keep others out, but now that he had a place of his own, he hoped the family would use the room with good thoughts about him. This exercise helped the family remember some good times, acknowledge some difficult times, and say good-bye in a positive way. Along with a few tears, a few smiles, and expressions of goodwill, the family was able to say a good good-bye.

A spiritual dimension can add richness to the ritual. Belief that God is at work in the life of the leaving-home member helps the family let go. We can surround that one with our prayers of God's blessing. We can covenant to be faithful prayer warriors. We can promise to remain emotionally connected through our correspondence and e-mails. While the empty bedroom will be a reminder of the loss, it can also be an impetus to prayer. When we lay in our beds, waiting to hear familiar footsteps coming up the stairs, we can ask for God's presence with our son or daughter wherever they are. When the absence leaves a silent sting that is too heavy to bear, we can write a letter, send a care package, or make an encouraging phone call. We can let them go with our blessing and with God's blessing.

Parents Are Human Too!

After the children leave home, for many the task is to live again as husband and wife without the children. For others, it is to live alone as a single adult. Shifts in the family brought about by the leaving will bring new and different challenges. Whatever pain and change this leaving home brings our way, it is also an opportunity for us and our families to grow in new directions. Praise God for the hope proclaimed in Jeremiah: "For surely I know the plans I have for you, says the LORD, plans for your welfare and not for harm, to give you a future with hope" (Jer. 29:11).

Two things can make for a better transition through the launching stage. One is for you to refocus on your marriage relationship. When your marriage is strong, the leaving-home process is easier. Take joy in recognizing a job well done and now focus on what's ahead. Try to support each other in every way possible. Rekindle your relationship. Make plans about joint projects. Take that trip you've been putting off.

Second, find new ways to open up your world. Take or teach a class, take up a new hobby or sport, join a support group. This is a time for you to come back into your life in a fuller way. You may feel lost at first, but making the effort will restore your vitality.

Rejoice! Your major parenting task is nearly done! You have moved your children from dependence, through independence, into interdependence. Trust God to work in and through them as they carve out their future.

Spiritual Implications

Remember when you first gazed at your newborn baby and began to dream dreams that would take him to wonderful and exotic places, that would give her an important life to live and an enormous purpose to fulfill? Now we put away the dreams that we dreamed for them so they can dream for themselves. But we can be assured that God has a plan and that they can look forward to a fulfilled life of their own.

When our (the Pipers') daughter Karlie thought she needed to "do" something challenging, she decided to go to Africa to work in a mission for four months. Of course, we asked all the usual questions one might ask in that situation: "Why Africa? Do you know how much disease is there? Do you know how unsafe those countries are? Do you know anything about this place?"

We were worried for her but also immensely impressed by her courage and her desire to serve. So for four months she was in the bush, working sixteen hours a day with children for a mission we knew nothing about. We could not call, and her letters arrived weeks after she had written them. And when they did arrive, they were not always so comforting. In one letter, she would talk of seeing the greatest amount of disease and poverty that she could imagine, and in the next talk of bungee jumping off Victoria Falls! There was only one thing that was certain. God knew where she was, and she was in his care.

We are so grateful that God gave us the courage to support her in this desire. What a life-changing experience it was for her, and how awful it would have been for us to limit her vision! As we went through the weeks of not knowing where she was, we learned to turn worry into prayer. After all, God was the only one with any power in the situation. What could our worry do?

There is so much to take to the Lord. Pray for the new independence they are seeking. Pray for their roommates, their professors, their employers, and their friends. Pray for their new church, their spiritual growth, and that they find a place to serve. Pray that they remember their roots and that they find their wings. What else is there to do? Can we bind them around us with an everlasting umbilical cord? Can we watch over them forever? Can we prepare the way for them as we did when they were young, keeping them forever dependent and prohibiting their growth? Of course not! The training has been done, the scaffolding has been removed, and the time has come for us to let them go.

Turning worry into prayer is a lifelong task. Most of us have had to learn to do this in many areas of life, not just with our children. Jesus clearly teaches us to trust our heavenly Father for what we need. Our task is to "seek first his kingdom and his righteousness" (Matt. 6:33 NIV). As we do that, God will provide.

Reflection Questions

1. Take fifteen to twenty minutes to reflect on the day you left home. Visualize the scene. Who was there? Take a minute to draw the scene on a piece of paper. Let your picture speak to you. What do you see? What emotions were you aware of? Share your picture with your spouse, a trusted friend, or your own family, and describe your leaving-home experience. Let it be a time of discussion as a family.

2. Ask your teenagers what they think would be a good leaving-home ritual. Create a ritual together that would be significant for the members of your family as you anticipate them leaving home.

10

Interpersonal Maturity with Adult Children

There are so many adjustments adult children have to make after they leave home. Apartment living means adjusting to a limited amount of space; living with a housemate, roommate, or spouse means adjusting to their ways of being; and dealing with the strangers who live next door means putting up with their barking dog. Yet most will work hard to adapt to their new surroundings and fit in the best way they can. They flex their independence muscles as they establish new boundaries with us and develop relationships apart from their family. So now where do we fit in?

Transitions are desirable yet disconcerting for us all. Even when we've given our blessing about the leaving, we may have apprehensions such as "Are they really ready? Is this the right choice for them? How will they manage without us? Will they find the right kind of friends?" While we worry about these types of things, our children may worry about losing their place in the family.

Many parents intentionally keep their kids' old rooms intact during the first year or two after their adult children are out of the home. This is a good omen indicating the family will not move on too quickly without them. In Gary's case, he left part of his belongings at home, just in case things did not work out with his new roommate. Jeanette asked her mother to help decorate the apartment she was sharing with her friend but didn't want to take anything from her bedroom at home. During this transitional time, it helps our kids to come back to the familiar, knowing they still have a special place in the family.

Needless to say, most young adults make the transition into adulthood, thriving on their choices and learning from their mistakes. They

153

meet the challenges, manage to weather the transitional storm, and do what it takes to cross over to the other side. The experience matures and prepares them to establish a belonging of their own. The question for us is how to interact with our adult children in ways that keep us connected while honoring their separation.

Home for the Holidays

We as parents manage to go on with our lives even though we miss our adult children who have left. But we eagerly anticipate their visits home, even if they live within a few miles of us. We have visions of the "good old days," when everyone is together again. And we tend to forget about the changes that have already occurred, which can make these visits less than ideal. Here's an example of the clashes that can happen during those much-anticipated reunions.

Julie, a young friend of ours, spent her first year away as an intern a thousand miles from home. Her first trip home came at Thanksgiving time, and her mother, Tina, was beside herself with excitement. Predictably, she baked all of Julie's favorite meals and treats in preparation for her arrival. In addition, she scheduled several family events that Julie had always loved doing. Tina was sure Julie would be delighted by all her efforts showing how glad she was to have her home.

Much to her chagrin, Tina was stunned by Julie's response! After the first few hours of Julie expressing how good it was to be home again, the honeymoon was over. During the meal that night, Julie announced she was on a low-fat diet and simply could not bring herself to eat those fat-laden foods her mother had so lovingly prepared. Then, to make things even worse, Julie wasn't sure she wanted to go to all those family gatherings. She had friends to see and places to go and didn't have time to do it all. And then there were irritating habits to tolerate as well, such as sleeping at odd hours and staying up half the night. "Who is this person?" Tina moaned. "She isn't the daughter who left home just four months ago. How could she have changed so drastically in such a short time?" With eagerness similar to what she had felt as she'd waited for Julie to come home, she now waited for her to leave so things could go back to normal!

Beware! Things have changed for everyone. The void left by the young adult's absence has been filled in other ways. The family has rearranged itself to deal with the gaps in order to find a new stability. We (the Pipers) remember the first Christmas vacation Aaron spent with us after going off to college. He hoped little had changed since his leaving. He wanted to watch every Christmas TV special the family had ever watched. He looked forward to traditional family outings, and he attended *The Nut-cracker* and *A Christmas Carol* with great enthusiasm. He hoped for every special meal to be prepared and all the old events to be held. It was important to him that many things stay constant.

But even though many things had stayed the same, he'd changed. It annoyed him that we wanted to know when he would be home and if he would be there for dinner. No one had asked him that for months. And we'd changed too. It was hard for him to be back in a family that had closed in the gap his leaving had created. So we needed to listen to each other and respect the changes that had occurred. In the process of talking together, we found ways to loosen up as well as maintain close relations.

Talk about these things ahead of time and make plans according to mutual preferences. Family life can be like a dance. Everyone must learn some different rhythms to enjoy a graceful new movement together.

Welcome to the Family

Our dreams for our children often come true when we stand at their side as they pledge themselves to their betrothed. However, once the honeymoon is over, we soon realize we must make some major adjustments. For a start, how are we to relate to this new family member? Supposedly, we have a new daughter or son, yet it doesn't really feel that way. We may be a bit uncertain about this relative stranger who has won our adult child's heart.

And there are other issues to deal with. Who will they spend the holidays with, or will they choose to be on their own? What traditions will they carry on, or will they create traditions of their own? How will we respond to these changes and our newest family member? What does it mean to be an in-law? What will the new spouse call us? How will we take on the mother-in-law/father-in-law role without becoming the dreaded outlaw? How can we assure the new couple that we want to be supportive, not intrusive?

James T. Burchaell makes an insightful comment: "The only home which is safe for anyone to be born into is the home that is ready to welcome someone who does not belong there by right of kinship, but belongs there in virtue of hospitality" (quoted in Clapp, 1993, p. 149). Can we be this generous as we accommodate new members into our families?

Developing a good relationship with a child's spouse is complicated but crucial. The intruding mother-in-law stereotype is alive and well. Most complaints of newly married couples have to do with an overinvolved mother or mother-in-law. In general, son-in-law/father-in-law relationships go along smoothly, unless the father feels his daughter is not being taken care of. The daughter-in-law/father-in-law relationship is most often a good-natured relationship. The mother-in-law/daughter-in-law and mother-in-law/son-in-law relationships seem to be the hardest to deal with.

So how do we welcome our son-in-law or daughter-in-law into the family? To say that we will treat this newest member as we treat our own children seems a bit naive. Many parents have annoying habits that their children tolerate because they love them. Hopefully our children have learned to ignore the unlovely in us. And because we have a long-standing relationship, we've weathered offenses on both sides and have come to an understanding that only time could produce. Our children's spouses don't share that history with us. This type of relationship is much more fragile and takes special care.

Let's look at the example of Debby, who thinks she has the greatest mother-in-law in the world. If Debby paints the living room, Mom O'Neill thinks she's done a great job. If Debby tries a new menu, Mom O'Neill thinks it tastes great. If Debby is overwhelmed with parenting, Mom O'Neill let's her know she believes in her ability to do it well and lends a hand. If Debby wants advice, Mom O'Neill will give that too but only if asked. In her consistent affirmation of Debby, Mom O'Neill has empowered her daughter-in-law.

Isn't this what we hope to do? To be a parent-in-law who is loving, affirming, and empowering? Of course, we don't want to add a burden of discontent in the first years of our children's marriages. We don't want to put our children in the awkward position of being pulled between their spouses and us. None of us wants to cause trouble, yet it can happen so easily.

The new couple needs to develop marital loyalty, strengthen their bond, and learn unique patterns of relating, and they do this best without our interference. The biblical idea of leaving parents to cleave to one's spouse clarifies the issue for us. We must win their trust and earn the right to enter into the relationship at their invitation. Our authority days are over.

And Then There Are Three!

Welcoming a baby into the world is actually a highly stressful time for most couples. The important thing for us as their parents is to be a resource during the time of adjustment. In addition, we're learning about our new role as well. What's involved in being grandparents? Will our children expect us to baby-sit, and will we meet the test when it comes to disciplining the grandkids? Although we might feel quite competent in the child-rearing department at this point, child-rearing practices have changed and our ideas might be considered out-of-date. Perhaps our children won't even want to hear our words of wisdom!

Let the new parents set the guidelines, but also let them know you're willing and eager to respond to their needs. Such things as taking the grandkids for an evening out, doing a few errands, bringing in a meal, or driving the grandkids to their appointments are loving gestures that can make a difference. We can lift our children's exhaustion by helping them with household matters such as painting a room, fixing the plumbing, or helping with spring-cleaning. We (the authors) know of grandparents who give one day or night a week so the couple has a regular date night. We know of other parents who pay for a yearly marriage enrichment weekend (as well as take care of the kids). These are all concrete ways to support the marriage.

Our Children's Children

Being a grandparent is one of life's richest blessings. As grandparents we have much to offer and pass down to the next generation. We have time to give. We can nurture, attend events, bring holiday cheer. We are reservoirs of family history and information. Grandparents who live far away must make every effort to stay connected if they want to be an influence in the lives of their grandchildren. If they don't, the children feel remote and distant when they visit. So bring an extra set of arms during the infant/toddler stages, do activities with school-aged grandchildren, be a nonjudgmental listener and self-esteem builder for teenage grandchildren. Grandparents can offer a perspective that softens the struggles between parents and their children. In fact, an intimate, meaningful relationship between grandparents and teenage grandchildren has been shown in studies to be mutually beneficial! So do everything you can to be there!

Who knows best? A recurring issue among grandparents who are highly involved with their grandchildren centers around discipline. It's easy to think "been there, done that," so you may run the risk of interfering. But be wise in your old age. Take the supportive role and follow these guidelines:

- Decisions rest with the parents
- Ask before assuming anything
- Consult parents before taking action

- Affirm the parents in front of their children
- Keep to the grandparent role

Whatever we do for our grandchildren must be done with their parents' approval. We can still get in trouble, even when offering help, if we do it in the wrong way. One grandmother decided to cut her granddaughter's long hair into a pixie style without consulting the child's mother. Understandably, this presumptuous act caused a serious breach. If we presume grandchildren are ours to do with as we please, we're sadly mistaken. They are not ours; they are our children's children, and it's the parents who must decide what's best. We must ask, offer, and invite, not assume, act, and demand.

Be creative and find special ways to relate to your grandchildren. We (the Balswicks) have made a practice of taking our grandsons on vacations. Whether it's taking a trip to the Rockies, crabbing at the ocean, learning to snorkel in Hawaii, climbing mountains in Tasmania, or backpacking through Europe, the grandsons bring enthusiasm to these wonderful adventures. The memories of these experiences will last a lifetime.

Single Adult Children

A twenty-eight-year-old single woman expressed having difficulty relating to her parents. In an attempt to resolve things, she invited them to a therapy session. In the session she tried to explain how it felt to be twenty-eight years old yet be treated like a child. In the middle of her explanation, her father interrupted her by saying, "Well, you are a child. You aren't even married yet!" Is that what it takes to qualify as an adult in parents' eyes? For many, apparently so. But that is an unfair burden to place on single adults. After all, not everyone gets married or has children. Those who are single are mature, worthy adults, and we must honor their singleness.

Just as we spoke of welcoming a spouse into our household, we also should welcome in the close friends of our adult children. Although adult singles may not have formed a family in the traditional sense, most have invested themselves in their work and significant relationships. Their support group includes special friends, a housemate(s), and church and community connections. Their living arrangements may be permanent or transitory, but they have established themselves as adults in their given community. We need to acknowledge their achievements, maturity, choices, and independent lifestyles. And we should let our actions reflect our belief that singleness is a God-ordained way of being in our world.

Our single adult children are independent adults who fully deserve our respect. Their life apart from us has a sacred boundary as well. We must not overstep the boundary or wear out our welcome. We must not undermine them with stereotyped messages. They need to be a vital part of our family gatherings, and we need to show appreciation for their contribution as a single member. We should always let them know how grateful we are for them.

The Single Parent

Some of our adult single children are parents. This may be the result of a death of a spouse, divorce, separation, or never-married status. The stress for the single parent can be enormous. Many find themselves in a situation they never bargained for or anticipated. Some parents may hesitate to lend a hand, thinking their children must prove they can do it on their own. Others step in and attempt to take over the single parent's life. But what we must do is support them in an empowering way.

Once again, the opportunity to be a positive influence in our children's lives presents itself to us. We don't want to take over or take on the responsibility of a second family, but we can make ourselves available in many ways. We must educate ourselves to the particular stresses of the single-parent home. We need to try to understand the consequences of traumatic distress on our adult children and our grandchildren. Experts identify the first two years following loss of a spouse as a crisis period for everyone involved. The intense emotional upset, economic hardship, and necessary readjustments are disruptive and disheartening—single parents have too little time, too few resources, and too few dollars, which puts considerable strain on the family. The relentless overload puts emotional pressure on the parent, along with the emotional ups and downs felt by all family members. Trying to put the pieces together usually is a bewildering task for grandchildren who are prone to worry about the future.

Children are resilient and usually make the necessary adjustments, so we can be an important resource in their lives that moves them in this direction. It is a challenge for us to know the best way to help, but making ourselves available is a good policy. Sometimes financial help may provide a stable environment that really makes a difference. We (the Balswicks) were able to provide this kind of help when our daughter went through her divorce. It allowed her and our grandchildren to remain in a stable environment while they were going through such drastic changes. Remaining in a familiar home, school system, and community can help ease the pain of the turmoil that is part of the separation/divorce. Frequent visits and being there during special celebrations such as birthdays and holidays are especially comforting in terms of emotional support. Life goes on, and some of these important traditions give a feeling of normalcy in the midst of abnormal changes.

Value System Challenges

You can't ever really anticipate how the choices your adult children make will impact your life, but they do! Each decision they make has potential for great happiness or great sadness, for them and often for you too. Sometimes you'll feel a bitter disappointment; other times you'll relish the wonderful successes of their life choices. No matter how old you are, you can be shattered by unfortunate decisions. So even when choices have the potential to rupture your relationship, how can you remain faithful through the hard times?

How often we the authors have had occasion to listen to parents agonize over the pain their children were "causing them." When a son moves in with his girlfriend, the response is often, "How could he do this to me!" Or when a daughter doesn't visit as much as the parents might like, they often take it personally. We tend to believe these actions are done *against* us (a form of rebellion) rather than simply being the result of a decision made out of a different value system. Some of our children's decisions may, indeed, be rebellion against God, but some may simply be a difference in preference. In either case, we do well not to personalize their decisions.

When we choose to view our children's decisions as persecutions directed at us, we are personalizing their actions. A daughter may not have considered us in the busyness of her life. A son may believe he is old enough to make a choice about his living arrangements. Considering our feelings may be no more than an afterthought, if that. Instead of playing the victim role, we should focus on how to preserve the relationship in a way that does not compromise our beliefs.

Finding Creative Solutions

An adult way to deal with adult children is to have a high regard for your relationship. Once a disagreement is recognized, declare the problem and commit to finding a solution together. The only solution may be for you to stay out of it, something parents have a hard time doing at any age! If conflict has been difficult for your family, admit dissatisfaction with past ways of dealing with conflicts and indicate a desire to try new ways of relating. Soften your approach as you offer hopeful possibilities of change. "I've been trying to force you into my way of doing things, but I know your way is equally good, and I will affirm you rather than criticize you." Or "I realize I keep my distance by blaming you, and I will accept responsibility for my actions from now on. It's important to me to find good ways to connect." Or "I don't agree with what you are doing here, but you are important to me and I am not willing to hurt our relationship over this." Honest communication and a vulnerable attitude initiate change possibilities. Here are some concrete suggestions:

- Acknowledge relationship strengths
- Work toward understanding
- Believe you can find a satisfactory resolution
- Choose to empower, not control
- Decide to accept, not shame
- Let go of unrealistic expectations
- Be hopeful; look for possibilities

If you can't get to a satisfactory resolution, you may have to address past hurts and misunderstandings. In this case, repentance and forgiveness will be a necessary part of the solution. Painful past events can continue to have a powerful negative effect unless you admit the wrongs and reestablish trust. After reconciliation, consider remedial efforts that will rebuild the relationship. There are times when a mediator/counselor can assist, so take the effort to call in a neutral person. A problem solved is a point of growth and celebration.

Parents Are Human Too!

We are now in the process of re-forming our lives after the children are grown and gone. For some of you, this is an exuberant time of life. You take great joy in the freedom of being on your own again. There is no one to answer to. There is more money to spend. You've done your job, and you're fancy-free. Even if you're still supporting adult children in some way, it's on your own time, not at their demand. There is now time to put full energy into your future.

For others of you, it may be a scary time, especially if you've tended to live your life through your children. You will be challenged to relate in new ways to your spouse or friends. There may be a season of depression and grief as you struggle to gain a new sense of purpose. This can be a particularly difficult time for women who have been stay-at-home moms and now face a lot of time on their hands. Single moms, as well, can feel especially alone in the isolation of an empty house.

Once again, changes are required of us as parents. Just when we settle in to sharing and sacrificing for our children, they disappear, and we are left with one more task to learn. For those of us who have been slowly letting go for the past several years, this seems like a natural next step. But for those who have resisted the letting-go process, it is painful.

We encourage you to step into this new phase of life with the same energy with which you embraced the task of becoming a parent. Step out, rejoice in what has gone before, and trust God. You have an opportunity to figure out how your life will unfold, and it's worth every minute and effort you take to come up with a proactive plan. Whether it's to revitalize your marriage or your life as a single adult, find a new vision for your future.

Adult children need us to take hold of our new lives now, so they will not have to worry about us and can fully commit to what is ahead for them. As they see us going on with our lives, they will be free to proceed with theirs. Parents who refuse to grow in their children's absence give the message that life without them is too difficult. It can be hard for adult children to be happy in their lives if our unhappiness carries over to them.

Spiritual Implications

We have many choices in how we re-form our lives for the future. As always, our task is to bring glory to Christ. Sometimes that will be easily and cheerfully done. At other times it will be a trial we would rather not face. Yet it is there for us to pursue. After all, God is not done with us yet. We should renew God's calling on our lives to express the love of Christ to those around us and demonstrate a way to live as godly people. We won't do it perfectly, of course, but with God as our guide, our strength, and our comfort, we'll be headed in the right direction.

This can be a wonderful time to increase our intimacy with God. While we have often pleaded with God on behalf of our children, we now have time to develop the more contemplative side of our relationship. Spending time and deepening our relationship with Christ is a rich benefit during the next years of our lives. So we should take time to be creative in establishing spiritual communion with our spouses, pray together for our children and grandchildren, and find a ministry to give ourselves to. We should also anticipate the new possibilities now that we have time to listen, to sit quietly before God, to bask in God's love, and to trust God in new ways. What a wonderful conclusion to a task completed!

Reflection Questions

1. Take a good look at what's happening between you and your adult children at this stage of life. Is there anything you want to do differently?
2. Indicate three proactive steps you can take to revitalize the relationship with your adult children.
3. What are some concrete things you can do to move toward reconciliation if there has been a misunderstanding between you? How will you know when things are resolved?

Part 3

Parenting As
a Godly Act

11

The Covenant Completed

Embedded in Community

We're familiar with the saying "It takes a village to raise a child." By now, we realize the Scriptures teach that the primary responsibility for rearing the child lies with the father and mother in the context of the family. Nevertheless, there is an essential community involvement. And for the Christian, that community is the covenant people of God, the church. In God's wisdom, the church is the community in which people, old and young, live and grow together. Even though the family has been idyllically portrayed as a refuge from a demanding world, it is truly a fragile unit, vulnerable to pressures outside of itself. We believe it is God's intent that the family be embedded in a broader community of faith.

Intended for Community

God wisely put children in families, and families in Christian communities. But we live in an age of fragmented families. Even "intact" families often don't have extended family members living anywhere close to them. And families that are isolated can easily be defeated. We believe it is crucial that families have the added resources of support that a Christian community offers. A church that not only provides corporate worship in spirit and in truth but also actively serves individuals and families of the congregation is living proof of covenant commitment. Being in such a community means our children have access to surrogate aunts and uncles, grandparents, adult friends, cousins and kin.

The family of God cares for its members by picking up the slack due to an overburdened single parent, by being there in sickness, during a birth of a child, when someone gets laid off at work, when someone moves or their house gets flooded, or during death and major crises. Church members can help celebrate the milestones, such as graduations, weddings, or even everyday events like ball games and concerts. Children growing up with many people involved in their lives feel loved in a way that will remain with them for a lifetime. When we take seriously the influence a peer group has on our kids, we'll be especially vigilant about participating in an active Christian community. Studies repeatedly have shown that regular church attendance keeps children and youth from many of the serious moral problems of the nonchurched. Church members are resources of inestimable value, and such a community provides a wide supply of support to families.

The body of Christ includes a whole host of individuals and families that make up the family of God. Whether single or married, young, middle-aged, or old, people covenant themselves to take an active role in the lives of all the members. In the family of God, we are bound together in love, and our unique gifts are given to us with the purpose of serving one another. First Corinthians 12 reminds us how each part is necessary for the healthy functioning of the whole. Each member contributes, whether it is the smallest child or the oldest adult. The foot is no less important than the hand, the eye no more important than the ear. How would we walk without feet, or hear without ears? And if we were all ears, how would we smell? We were made to live in community, with the hands drawing on the gifts of the eyes, and the feet working together with the legs. Our connection is vital if we want to function as a whole and healthy body.

So what role does our church have in the raising of our children? To be sure, the roles of church and family are different, yet when a child is baptized or dedicated, those present at that event (the church) vow to pray for, encourage, and care for the child being presented. How seriously have you taken that vow that you've assented to on numerous occasions? Is it just part of the liturgy that goes in one ear and out the other? And exactly what kind of involvement does it require?

As we (the Pipers) look at our church calendar for the weekend, we see that a teenager has a varsity volleyball game on Friday night. We've decided to attend, and we know that many from the church will be there to support her. Last year there were about fifteen people from the church at one of Kelsey's games. One of her teammates asked her if all those people were related to her, and Kelsey responded, "Well, sort of . . . that's my church." When a church community surrounds their children with such commitment, it gives the children a secure place of belonging.

Relationship-Empowering Congregation

The driving force behind covenant is accountability, care, and service. We believe that a vital church community will practice relationship-empowering principles just as the vital family does. What makes a church a relationship-empowering community? Of course, Jesus Christ being honored and exalted is primary. But three other areas come to mind to help answer that question: safety, caring connection, and hope. There are perhaps many others we could add to the list, but here we'll address these three essential components.

Safety

One of the most important things for children to know is that their community is a safe place—physically, spiritually, and emotionally safe. Of course, all of us do all we can to make sure that our children are in no physical danger while involved in the church. Yet we have heard stories of children not feeling safe, babies not being well cared for in the nursery, teenagers being humiliated by a Sunday school teacher, or other horror stories we hate to hear. Safety is a primary requirement.

Pay attention to whether your children are spiritually safe as well. Make sure they are in an environment where questions are taken seriously and true faith is encouraged. When children are expected to believe without being allowed to question, their faith does not become their own. As children develop their minds, they naturally will have many questions to ask. Church needs to be a safe place to discuss these weighty matters.

Emotional safety includes making sure the church is a place where children are allowed to be children and where they are protected from inappropriate judgments or expectations. They should not be discouraged with comments such as, "I'm ashamed of you—you're supposed to be a Christian!" or "You've been a bad influence on the other kids!" or "And to think that your parents are leaders in the church and you did that!" These hurtful statements stick with a child for years to come.

Children and teens need the emotional safety of not being judged. In our (the Pipers') church there is a teenager who comes to church each week with the most amazing hair coloring! Sometimes it is red and black, sometimes green and orange, sometimes pink and purple. Who knows what color Jeana's hair will be next! But she is never judged by it. Jeana's hair and punk clothing are her way of being uniquely herself, and we all know it. She is a believer and is committed to Christ and to service in her congregation, and we feel so blessed that she is a part of us! How

different it might be for her if she didn't feel loved and accepted, no matter what her hair color or clothes. That too is emotional safety. We also
keep children safe by equipping, training, and helping them become
competent, responsible, and accountable using clear standards and guidance that provide a solid foundation of growth.

Besides being a supportive community, the church also serves as an
accountable presence for both parents and children. Children who are
integrated into the care of the congregation are accountable to it.

Caring Connection

Your children should be confident that church is a place where others really care about them. This can be shown in many ways. Adult members can commit to praying regularly for and taking an interest in a specific child. Remembering children on birthdays and holidays, mailing
a card once a month to let them know you are thinking of them, or
affirming them each Sunday in some concrete way brings a special connection with them. Children naturally respond to those who take time
to know them and take their concerns seriously.

Showing up at special events is another concrete way to demonstrate
caring. Going out of your way to attend sporting events and concerts or
simply dropping by a teen's place of work increases the level of connection, because you've gone out of your way to get to know them.
Finally, the church can encourage the faith of children and youth by
supporting mission trips, dinners, and fund-raisers. Whether a congregation is large or small, what it takes is a covenant commitment to follow through in a meaningful way.

A Place of Hope

A body of believers that provides a safe place of belonging and truly
cares for its children will become a place of hope and vision. It's not
only the prayers but also the vision a congregation holds out for its children as they struggle through their journeys of faith that empowers. If
we come alongside them during their joys as well as their disappointments, we can bring them spiritual encouragement. When we let them
know we take seriously the vows we made at their baptism or dedica-
tion, we hold out the hope that they will follow Christ throughout their
lives and take their place with God's people. To the extent that the congregation is a safe place of acceptance, an intimate connection of care,
and provides a hopeful vision of the future, the church will be a powerful force of accountability in the lives of parents and children.

Relationship-Empowerment Principles in Community

The REP model is based on four relationship principles modeled by God in the Bible: (1) covenant, a commitment of unconditional love; (2) grace, a commitment of acceptance and forgiveness; (3) empowerment, a commitment of service and submission; and (4) intimacy, a commitment of knowing and being known. Here we apply these biblical principles to the Christian community.

A Covenant Community

A covenant commitment is more than saying words; it is doing what we say we will do. Covenant love says we will be faithfully present and predictable to those in our community. We can be counted on not only to show up but also to keep the pledges we make to each other. We will show love in our actions toward others and seek their good and growth. Covenanting together in community is a commitment to stay with people through the hard times. When families know that the church community stands with them when things get tough, they can deal with the difficulties that are part of each family's life.

Finding a church that has covenanted together in community is a real blessing. It establishes ties to a community of believers with whom we can share our joys as well as our sorrows.

A Gracing Community

Offering grace has to do with accepting others into our community without hesitation or reservation. Differences tend to raise bristles even when we know that diversity is good for us. But grace requires that we value differences and praise God for how it broadens our community. When we accept children, youth, and families with the grace we are shown by Christ, we refrain from trying to make them acceptable to us. Grace allows us to embrace others "as they are" and to give them the benefit of the doubt. It helps us treat others with the same mercy our Lord extends to us.

A friend recently explained why she had left her church. In the past year, her daughter had a baby out of wedlock and gave the baby up for adoption. Her church was pretty quiet on the subject, most of the time acting as if it wasn't happening. She tried talking with some of the women about her pain but felt judged by their responses. Finally, she decided she didn't want to continue being the one with the "messed-up daughter."

Belonging to a church where people are accepting, generous, tenderhearted, and merciful brings healing. A community that seeks to reconcile is one where members bear with one another and practice forgiveness. Colossians 3:12–15 gives us a taste of what it's like to be in a community marked by grace.

> As God's chosen ones, holy and beloved, clothe yourselves with compassion, kindness, humility, meekness, and patience. Bear with one another and, if anyone has a complaint against another, forgive each other; just as the Lord has forgiven you, so you also must forgive. Above all, clothe yourselves with love, which binds everything together in perfect harmony. And let the peace of Christ rule in your hearts, to which indeed you were called in the one body.

An Empowering Community

Empowerment in Christian community has to do with actively investing ourselves in the lives of our members. Sunday school teachers, church leaders, pastors, and members play an important part in faith development and spiritual growth. So does teaching, modeling, equipping, encouraging, and helping others reach their fullest God-given potential. Loving confrontation and challenge keeps us accountable to striving toward God's transforming power in our lives.

Empowerment involves surrendering self-centered goals in order to build up others. As each member is nurtured, empowered, and transformed into the image of Christ, the whole community becomes strong and effective. To do this we must serve each other with our gifts, which are varied. A young child can bring a smile to an elderly person, a choir of children's voices can be an inspirational part of worship, a group of teenagers can open our eyes to needs in our communities as they serve the homeless. No member is more important than any other member. By showing our children and youth we value them, we encourage them to develop their gifts in the context of serving others.

A few years ago, a young family in our (the Pipers') church had a tough decision to make regarding employment. The whole congregation prayed with the family and agonized as they did, struggling to know the will of God. At last the decision was made, and everyone rejoiced to find that they were staying in the area. Many were aware of the sacrifice they were making to remain in Seattle. The biggest loss was not being close to their family.

In an attempt to truly live out a community, our church had a party and gave them a gift of love. It was a box of coupons, written by church members on slips of paper redeemable throughout the year. A teenage boy named Josh would take four-year-old Kevin to a movie of his choice once a month. Kelsey would have Danielle spend the night with her every other month. Another couple would take the children for the weekend so the parents could get away. Megan would baby-sit whenever needed. Karen would be there regularly on Tuesdays to give Jo a time to do her exercise class. There were invitations to dinner, dessert surprises, drivers, etc. The congregation showed their appreciation to God by loving this family as only the family of God can do.

An Intimate Community

Being known is a necessary part of community belonging. We long to be understood, especially when we are in pain. Parents need a place where their concerns about their children can be openly received. Children and youth need to know that their church family will take the issues they face seriously. Hopefully, we will have family, friends, and support groups in the churches we attend. These relationships will be the crux of our being known in our community.

It is mind-boggling to think that the all-knowing, all-powerful, transcendent God wants to know us and commune with us. The fact that the deep mysteries of God have been expressed through a human—Christ—puzzles us. And yet this is precisely what the Scriptures tell us about our Creator God. We are invited to commune with and know Jesus in intimate ways. In the process of knowing God, we come to know how to be more fully ourselves in God's image. As a community of image bearers, we are capable of authentic interactions with each other that reflect this image.

Intimacy in a congregation often comes through small group interaction. A small group is a safe place where we can let others know us, as well as get to know other congregants at a deeper level. It takes vulnerability and humility to take down our protective cover and let others see us as we are. When we are willing to admit mistakes and deal with our failures, our kids will be more open about their struggles and ask for help. When we strip off our pretenses, we can be more accountable to ourselves, God, and others. So often kids see hypocrisy in the church, but when they see genuine confession, people being open with each other, making amends, and restoring relationships, it makes a huge impression.

Church Members Are Human Too!

Although we long to be in a relationship-empowering community, we are not all so fortunate to experience our churches in that way. Criticism, slander, impatience, and conformity are strong forces in many parts of Christ's body. In situations colored by these things, we do not feel safe, and rightly so, because these attitudes are not conducive to safety. Fear is the culprit that keeps us from being known in this type of community. Fear of being exposed, rejected, attacked, ignored, or overwhelmed prevents us from telling our true stories. It's easier to present the self we think is acceptable.

When a congregation expects conformity, it is tempting to keep ourselves hidden. We master the technique of impression management and present untruths and false fronts, which keep distance between others and ourselves. Then the church becomes a hotbed of denial that hinders growth, and pointing fingers and blaming becomes an insidious way of dodging "self" truth.

It's bizarre to realize that the church sometimes has become the last place where people can be truthful. Our automatic response is to hide hurts and struggles, because we fear that when we're honest, we'll be told, "Forget it—that's over now. You are a new creature in Christ, so get on with it." But we need to be able to talk about the times we really blow it as parents! We need to share our concerns about our teenagers and what they're involved in, to ask prayer for our unmarried pregnant daughter or unbelieving son as we support them during a difficult time.

Dealing with Our Differences

There are several areas that tend to cause problems for families living in close community. Because we are imperfect in our knowledge of Christ and of biblical interpretation, it is inevitable that we will bring different perspectives to our communities of faith. How quiet does a child need to be in a worship service? What is correct discipline? Which clothing styles are permissible? And so on. So when our children ask why eight-year-old Johnny gets to watch PG movies, or why Kathy doesn't have to wear a dress to worship, or why the Rogers family gets to go to a baseball game on Sunday, it can be tough.

Differences among church members are natural. Christians, all trying to live godly lives of obedience, have differences of opinion on various issues. This is a fundamental lesson for our children. And how we as adults respond to these differences is even more critical. If we respond with negativity toward our brothers and sisters in Christ, our children will observe this and learn from it. If we question a person's faith, if we gossip, exalt ourselves, and portray the other family as less than us, we are setting an example that our children will most likely follow.

Here are some guidelines for dealing with church-family differences.

- Be Christlike! We are being observed by our children
- Be respectful about differences in parenting decisions
- Be nondefensive and give reasons behind your decision making
- Attend parenting groups to discuss values and specific problems together
- Make creative plans with other parents for prom nights, etc.

However it is done, the church needs to be at the forefront in providing parents with the opportunity to learn from each other and to increase their understanding of their children and their role as parents. Only the church has the capacity to approach this sensitive area with trust in God's wisdom. And when our children and teens see Christlike characteristics modeled in their community, they are more likely to take on godly attributes.

Spiritual Implications

In community we build a beautiful tapestry of our lives together as families within the family of God. God is the source of our belonging and hope; Jesus gives us a vision of something beyond ourselves. We make our peace with one another through God's love so generously given, through Christ's forgiveness so graciously offered, and through the Holy Spirit so freely empowering.

Our God is a God who walks with us even through the valley of the shadow of death, and we are expected to do the same with one another. God binds up our wounds, heals our broken hearts, carries our burdens, and empowers us to move toward wholeness. We are called to do the same. The community of faith, where God's Spirit dwells, is our main hope for health and family support. And in our continued humanness, we have the promise of forgiveness, reconciliation, and hope.

Reflection Questions

1. Evaluate your church in the areas of safety, genuine caring, and hopeful vision for the future, in regard to children. How might you help improve these areas?
2. How might you draw upon the family of God to meet some of your family needs?

3. Review how children are treated in your church. What do they learn about God, God's people, themselves, and their future from being part of your congregation?
4. What opportunities for growth and service are there for children in your church?

12

Regenerative Parenting

A Life-giving Privilege

We have brought forth life, and being parents has been a life-giving privilege. But even more than this, the relationship-empowering dynamics will dramatically change us. Being challenged to work out our relationships with our children in godly ways will transform us into more godly persons. Parenting then becomes a spiritual act, a sacred journey.

At this juncture in the book, we the authors would like to tell our personal stories of transformation. In a nutshell, the relational God who created us to be relational beings has used our parent/child relationships to transform us. The normal tension of everyday family life as well as the extraordinary anxiety of major crises throughout life stages has changed us. We have had to face our sinful natures as never before. We have had to learn to sacrifice and give ourselves unconditionally; to accept and embrace our differences and ask for forgiveness seventy times seven; to face conflicts and tolerate the unknown; to take down our pretenses and be honest and vulnerable; and to admit our failures and express our deepest longings and hurts. Yes, we have been changed! Not in an instant, but through the lifelong process of parenting, a refining experience. The parent/child encounter has smoothed out some of our rough edges and made our crooked paths straight.

Our biblical model claims that the act of parenting can be a regenerative process. Our hope is that you'll find our personal musings about our humorous foibles and serious struggles to be enlightening and spiritually challenging. We trust you will see how using personal power *for* the relationship is the guiding force behind empowerment.

Judy's Journey

I begin with what my firstborn child, Jacque, taught me, a new mother, about myself. She was a beautiful child with amazing energy and a strong will. But these things tapped into one of my problem areas, which was control. I'd never realized how one small child could trigger such deep feelings in me whenever our encounters took us in an "out of control" direction.

Tantrums were part of my first refining process. When I used the bossy mother tactic—demanding that she take a nap, hurrying her into the car because I was late, or refusing a reasonable request—it predictably failed. She countered with the only thing she knew, which was to refuse to give in to me. And what's worse, I knew there was no way I really could control these things. I could not make her sleep, or move her faster than she could go, or explain my refusal to her satisfaction. These maneuvers only exasperated her and defeated me.

Many times I went to Jack with my teary stories, feeling discouraged by Jacque's tantrums. He was good about listening and supporting me with compassion but also helped me look more deeply at my controlling ways. This brought me to my knees in prayer more than I'd like to admit! But I needed to bring this tendency under control before the Lord. It was a humbling experience to be broken and admit I needed to change. However, once I examined the fears behind my controlling behavior, I could face myself for real.

Healing brought change. I was able to soften my approach, make use of natural and logical consequences, and remove myself from the power struggles. Then Jacque was free to be who she was without such a need to resist me. And I had more regard for her unique personality by learning to work *with* her rather than *against* her. This change didn't happen overnight, and I still struggle with control issues, but Jacque's persistence in being herself gave me the opportunity to be more empowering in all my relationships.

My son Jeff was a delightful, easygoing child. He brought humor and a fun-loving personality into our family. But there were times when he could really get my goat. For instance, one day when he lied to me, I felt as if I had been hit at the core of my being. My sweet child had just told a bold-faced lie! I remember yelling at him at the top of my voice. As I picture it now, I see this angry mother bearing down like a big, dark monster on a scared little boy.

A year later, after Jeff's cancer surgery and recovery at Bethesda Hospital in Maryland, I sat in the motel room with him, watching a Sunday-morning preacher on TV. The preacher made a statement that impacted me during this very sad time in our lives. He said that it would radically change family relationships if we would turn to each other every day and say, "I forgive you, do you forgive me?" This hit me like a ton of bricks—immediately that scene of me scolding Jeff came into view. I turned the TV off and said those exact words to Jeff. I told him how sorry I was for the time I had so ruthlessly laid into him. He was quick to say back, "Oh, Mom, I forgive you, do you forgive me?" Both of us had done wrong, and a nine-year-old boy was able to forgive and be forgiven. That intimate moment brought a healing bond between us that remains with me to this day.

We do things each day in our family relationships that need to be forgiven, and making forgiveness an everyday practice is a way to keep the slate clean. That moment between Jeff and me changed me at a deep level! From then on, I decided to center on Christ and stop the emotional outbursts. I knew that once I was calm, I could choose to be different. And instead of letting circumstances bring out the worst in me, I was able to bring my best to the circumstances. This was a million-dollar lesson in relationships.

It's certainly been a joy to have our adopted son, Joel, as part of our family. We never could have imagined how much he would give to each one of us. Arriving in our home at ten years of age was not an easy feat for him, or for our family. Each of us had some major changes to make, so we sought help from a family therapist. Joel had no idea what he was getting into, and we had no idea how much God was going to use him to change us. But that's what happened.

I guess the biggest stretch for me was opening up my heart to Joel, especially when his guard was up. "How will I ever get through!" I cried to God at night. Joel had taken a huge risk coming to the U.S., after surviving several orphanages and living in the streets of Seoul for years. At one level, it seemed as if he didn't need us, but on another level, he was desperate for love. I wanted so badly for him to know he belonged to us and that we would never let him go. But this was going to take time.

Jack and I believed that God had given us a special sign to help us in our doubts, which we still hold on to. Joel put his foot down on U.S. soil on the exact anniversary of Jeff's death. The day before we got Joel, we had received a phone call in Georgia telling us to meet the plane from Korea, and we excitedly and hurriedly got our things together. On the plane to O'Hare Airport, where we would be picking up Joel, Jack and I looked at each other, remembering what day it was. It was like God was telling us he would see us through it all and that everything would be okay. We knew we would have to open ourselves up to Joel and that he would have to learn to trust us.

But the process was difficult. Sometimes I wondered if he would ever bond with me. Sometimes I wondered if he was angry with me or just fearful of being abandoned again. These and many more were the questions and doubts in my mind.

A year later, when our family had a chance to spend nine months in Seoul, I was very anxious. Maybe Joel would run away from us, and we would never find him in that big city! This took more trusting in God. But God answered my prayers on the plane flight to Korea, when Joel asked me a question I will never forget: "What will happen if I get lost in Seoul? How will anyone know you are my mother?" There was my sign—he didn't want to lose us any more than we wanted to lose him! "Thank you, Jesus!" was my response. Yes, I had been challenged to trust God in all things, but God had given me a promise I could hold on to. It was a transforming lesson in my spiritual journey.

Boni's Journey

I remember a comment a friend made to me when she observed me with my firstborn child: "You don't just love Aaron; you seem to adore him!" And I did. I thought he was the greatest little kid ever born. And I was terrified I was going to mess him up. Coming from an alcoholic family, I felt I knew nothing about being a good parent, let alone a Christian one. But I had my love.

Love enables you to do things you don't want to do. It empowers you to look outside yourself and see things from the perspective of the other, to fight for the good of someone else, to go a second or third mile if necessary. This kind of love that I had for Aaron, and then for Karlie and Sarah when they came along, empowered me to try to figure out how to be a better parent.

Nothing in my life causes me more grief than the mistakes I know I have made as a parent. I have done many things wrong, and many things right as well, but I sure remember the wrongs more than the rights. I have learned a lot along the way and often wish I knew then what I know now. But if I had to choose one thing that parenting did for me, I would say that it forced me to grow. I grew in my relationship with Christ and in my development of a healthy self. God used my children to help me in this.

I so wanted a boy when I was pregnant with Aaron. I come from a Middle Eastern culture, where boys are everything. And to have my firstborn be a boy seemed the tops to me. My husband hoped for a girl, however. He had fallen in love with his two-year-old niece a few years before and hoped to have a "Julie" duplicate. But a boy it was, and we were both thrilled. I think for me this desire for a son was deeper than the influence of my culture. I was fearful of raising daughters. My husband was such a good man—he could be in charge of raising sons, so I would be less needed. Girls! What did I know of girls! Being a person who did not feel good about herself, I was afraid of not being a good enough role model for a daughter. I thought having all boys was the way to go.

But God gave me two daughters, and once again I'm so glad God didn't take my fears or requests too seriously. I love having daughters! I especially love having adult daughters and am so thankful for the friendships I have with Karlie and Sarah. Again it was love at first sight with each of them, and that love has carried us through some hard times. Somewhere in me I knew it was the *relationship* between my children and me that was the crux of good parenting. God modeled that for me and applied it to my heart in regard to my children. So the REP model has been there for quite a while, longing to be fleshed out.

Parenting has brought me more joy than any one person should have! I loved being with my kids, loved the family trips, loved the enthusiasm of an evening out. I remember the fun times when we discovered (before VCRs) that we could rent movies at the library, borrow the projector from the church, and have movies in our home. Popcorn and Coke and friends and a movie too! That was living! And I loved hearing Aaron play the French horn and watching the girls play volleyball. I was their greatest fan, which was sometimes a little more than they could take!

But there was pain too. Parenting took a toll on my body. I was often exhausted and frazzled by the amount of work three kids demanded of me. I also remember the pain of seeing one of the children getting made fun of by other kids, seeing another getting their heart broken in the teen years, and seeing another missing out on a job as a young adult. I don't handle the pain of my children very well. It was always a struggle to let them feel the pain, to allow the natural consequences to take their course. Don has likened me to a lioness protecting her cubs, and I know exactly what he means when he says that. I constantly work at holding it in, at getting out of the way, at not being too big in their lives.

Therapists call this blurring of emotional boundaries "enmeshment." It's not a good thing to be enmeshed with your kids. It makes you say dumb stuff such as, "I'm cold, put a coat on" or "I'm tired, go to bed." But knowing you're doing this helps, and working to allow children to have their own thoughts and feelings can be successful.

It took a differentiated self for me to make real headway in this area. Differentiation means being able to allow for a separateness between yourself and another person. To be able to feel okay when people don't think and feel like you do, to not depend on others to make things okay, and to not feel driven to make everything okay for everyone else. As I worked year after year to become healthier in my relationship to my own parents, I was more able to encourage differentiation in my children. I also grew in my relationship to God and in my knowledge of the Holy Spirit at work in my children and me. Once I began to grow in affirming their separate selves, I became fearful of what they would do with that separateness. The truth of God in their lives allows me to rest and to see the wonderful people that they are.

I still get on Aaron a lot. I guess it's the oldest-child thing, or maybe it's the Middle-Eastern-mother-with-a-son thing. Or maybe it's just that he is so good-natured about it when I do get on him! Aaron has a very forgiving heart and cuts me a lot of slack. He is his dad's best friend and a delight to both his parents—a man of God with a soft heart, humble spirit, and constant integrity. I love him, as I always have.

Don and I used to think that Karlie and Aaron were as different as night and day, but they grow more like each other the older they get. Karlie has a very sensitive heart for those in need. She is compassionate, loving, godly, and courageous. Sometimes I look at her and marvel at the potential God has given her, and I thank him that he gave me this wonderful daughter.

Sarah is an empowered young woman. More than any person I have ever met, Sarah has the ability to know what she wants and to make it happen. That she is able to do this with grace, compassion for others, and integrity is a testimony to her love and commitment to God. What a joy she is!

Not a day goes by that I do not thank God for letting me walk this life with my children. They have taught me so much, and I now have the joy of calling them friends. And Don has been my lifelong partner, co-laborer, and often teacher in this walk. My children have had a wonderful father in every respect. He has been our rock and our model of unconditional love here on earth.

My testimony to parents is to encourage them to be able to look past what is familiar and comforting in parenting styles and to look to the model that God holds out to us. Do the work of making changes to align yourself with God's model for parents. Separating your issues and working on them is good for your kids. Your growth as a healthy, God-empowered person is a gift that goes on giving in your life and in theirs.

Jack's Journey

As is the case with most parents, I sometimes doubted how effective I was as a parent. This was especially true when my daughter, Jacque, went through some of the usual types of rebellion. Thus it was surprising to overhear this advice she, as a young married mother, gave to her brother Joel when he was a teenager: "You better listen to Mom and Dad because they know more than you do!" I remember thinking, "Is this the same person who was my defiant teenage daughter a few years ago?"

Jacque went on to earn her college degree in child development, and she put this to good use as a director of a day care center for children. It was with a combination of pride and amazement that I observed the wisdom she showed in dealing with large numbers of children. I was particularly impressed with her patience, her ability to settle conflicts between children, and her wonderful capacity to affirm and make each child feel special.

Jacque is now a mother of four boys ranging in age from two to seventeen. If the criterion for success as a parent is for your own children to be effective parents, Judy and I have accomplished something. I think Jacque is a wonderful mother, showing her boys the right combination of guidance and freedom, love and discipline, expectations and support.

As a grandfather, one of my greatest delights has been doing active things with my grandsons. What lets me know that Jacque appreciates my parenting ability is that she has shown complete confidence in me when I'm with her boys. This includes caring for three-year-old Taylor, responding to two-year-old Liam when he wants "Bampie" to read him a story, and doing somewhat risky activities (motorcycle riding, surfing, snowboarding, rock climbing) with the big guys, Curt and Jake, ages sixteen and seventeen. I can't remember her even once questioning my behavior with her boys. The privilege of being actively engaged with her sons has been a sweet joy in my life as a grandfather.

For ten years I was privileged to have a son who was warm, loving, and expressive of his feelings. Jeff died a few days short of his tenth birthday, after a four-month fight with cancer. My warmest memories of Jeff are the times we enjoyed being close at bedtime. I established a ritual with him in which I would tuck him into bed, talk about his day, and then, before turning off the lights, tell him that I loved him. He would invariably reply, "I love you too, Dad." Sometimes he'd beat me to the punch and would say, "I love you, Dad" before I had a chance to tell him first.

But our relationship hadn't always been so close. Until four years earlier, I had devoted so much time to my work as an assistant professor that I had little quality time left for fathering. The change came when Judy began to work on her doctoral degree. I really became a coparent at this point in our family life. I would be home at 3:30 each afternoon to meet the kids when they got off the school bus, help them with their homework, fix dinner, and welcome Judy home after a long day of classes.

As I look back now, I truly consider this change a blessing in disguise. Some of my colleagues teased me about being a househusband, but putting a priority on my family reaped rich rewards. In fact, after my son's death, I would often think about how sad it would have been had I not spent this extra time with my children. They got quality attention from me, and I got close to them. Now that I was a more involved parent, they came to me when they were hurt or scared, and I opened up emotionally as a result. The vulnerability they shared gave me a chance to connect with them at a deep level. The death of my son is made bearable by the four years we had expressing our mutual love.

A few days after Jeff's death, Judy and I were cleaning out his dresser drawers and found a note he had written to us sometime in the past. The note said, "I love you, Mom and Dad, even when you get mad at me. I will always love you." As I reflect on the closeness of our relationship, I thank God for using circumstance to develop me beyond the shallow father I had been into one who could regularly say "I love you" to my children.

Our son Joel was ten when we adopted him. He was an excellent soccer player, but after trying to bond with him playing with my limited soccer skills, I decided that teaching him to play tennis was a good idea. It was a sport I was fairly good at. And, being a good athlete, Joel quickly learned the sport. By the time he was fifteen he was giving me some hard matches. But I still could usually win, and that felt good, especially since I was just beginning my midlife stage. At age seventeen, Joel's skill continued to improve as he played on the high school tennis team. To say that he could give me a good game is an understatement.

I remember one day when we were playing and he was beating me pretty bad. I was becoming increasingly frustrated when I realized that this son whom I had taught to play tennis was beating me at my own game. Right after he drove a hard volley to the left corner of the baseline, the frustration got the best of me. I was ready to give up since I couldn't clobber him at the game. But then I reflected on my emotional state and remembered the concept of empowerment that I taught in my classes. I looked at my talented son and was so proud of him. Then I said to myself, "Jack, you're a fantastic coach!" Ha! This reframe saved the day.

I'm still a competitive player, but I can relax and be glad for his accomplishments now. My son not only became an excellent tennis player, but he also opened up a tennis shop after graduating college and coached high school tennis. In fact, the concept of mutual empowerment was evident, because he began giving me tips about how to hold my forehand to get a better serve. I was delighted to realize that my son was now empowering me! Through Joel I had come to realize that what God intends for a parent/child relationship is a mutually empowering experience. What a privilege it is!

Don's Journey

The first time Boni told me I was going to be a father, I was shocked. I hadn't given much thought to having children or to raising them. I was happy just being with Boni and being a couple. I feared that a child would interfere with our happiness. Perhaps that is part of the reason why we were using birth control when she got pregnant. But six months into the pregnancy, we lost the baby in a harrowing experience. Boni was devastated. I felt very little—except for some guilt for feeling very little.

So three years later, when Boni again told me she was pregnant, and again we were using birth control, I became anxious. I feared that because I was ambivalent about having a child, God might take it away again. And if he didn't and the baby was born, I was concerned that I would not love it properly.

I hoped the baby would be a girl, because I had a niece named Julie whom I dearly loved, and I knew how to show affection to a girl. I was concerned about whether or not I could love a little boy. Boni, who is always encouraging me, assured me that I could, but I wasn't so sure. I knew I could enjoy sports with him. I knew I could teach him right from wrong. But I was worried about showing affection to a boy. Could I hug a little boy? Could I kiss a little boy? Would I want to?

But God prepared me. While these concerns were still in my mind as my son was being born, the moment I saw him, my heart melted. I wept with joy, partly because he began breathing after not breathing for seven minutes. Within two minutes of his breathing, I was holding him and cuddling him. From that day on, I held him and hugged him and kissed him and wrestled with him without thought. It was natural. God, through Aaron, my son, brought out a love in me that I didn't know existed.

When Karlie arrived two years later, I was ready—I thought. I was ready to hold and cuddle and kiss. But Karlie was never much interested in cuddling. Boni, in her wisdom, made me responsible for Karlie's early-morning feeding. I would sit and hold her and look deeply into her eyes. And she would search mine as she drank from her bottle. In those quiet early-morning hours, Karlie taught me a silent love that was overwhelming.

When Sarah came into our home at age six months, I secretly wondered if I could love her the same way I did my two biological children. And if I did, I wondered if I would be able to express it outwardly. Within minutes of seeing her at the airport, all doubt vanished. I wanted to hold her and cuddle her so badly that my arms ached. She was so full of smiles and hugs that I could not hold back even if I'd wanted to.

God, through all three children, brought out love in me and taught me how to express it. Where before I had been undemonstrative, I became demonstrative without thought. From day one, each child taught me how to be affectionate and how to physically and emotionally relate to children, whether male or female.

I also learned about the deeper issues of life from them. Before I had children of my own, I was often critical of parents who were not consistent in their discipline. It irked me when parents would say "no" four or five times in a row to children who would continue to disobey. I wanted children who would obey, and I knew that immediate and consistent discipline would be effective. I also was disturbed by children who seemed to have no regard for other people's property and was dismayed when parents seemed oblivious as their children tore around homes and damaged all kinds of objects. I believed that my children would learn respect for property.

While I still believe consistency in discipline is important, and while I still believe children should learn respect for property, in one incident, I learned a deeper truth with respect to both. I learned patience and mercy.

One day when I was going over to my office at the church building, which was just across the street from our house, Aaron, who was in kindergarten at the time, asked if he could come along. I told him that he could if he could play quietly while I worked. When we got to my office, I gave him some paper and crayons, and he sat on the floor and began to draw quietly. After about thirty minutes, I looked down and saw that he was no longer drawing on the paper I had given him but was scribbling on the manila folder that I kept committee minutes in. I reacted in anger and scolded him. While he looked up at me with big, sad, brown eyes, I lectured him about respect for other people's property. Then I sent him home with tears flowing down his face. Later when I was finished with my work, I picked up the folder from the floor and noticed that his scribblings actually formed words. There, written on a lousy, five-cent folder, in large, wobbly, kindergarten scrawl, were the words "I LOVE YOU DAD." You can only imagine how I felt. I still have that folder—twenty-five years later. I keep it as a reminder of the weightier matters my son taught me that day.

Through this one painful situation I learned what Jesus sought to teach the Pharisees. Jesus never criticized them for keeping the details of the law. But he criticized them for neglecting mercy (Matt. 23:23). Should I teach my children to obey? Yes. Should I teach them to respect property? Yes. But my children have taught me over and over again to remember to look at the big picture, to remember the weightier matters of love, mercy, and patience.

Personal Reflections

We feel enormously blessed to have our adult children as friends. We have all grown in the process of learning to see the world from each other's perspectives. We have learned to negotiate and believe that when we want what is best for each one, it puts us on the same team. It's a great feeling! Yet our work is not done. Thank goodness our relationships continue to grow. And we've expanded our relationships to include a daughter-in-law and sons-in-law and grandchildren. We hope to be an empowering presence in their lives always. And we will do our part, which is to keep our marriages strong and be available when they call.

We give the best we have to give, yet sometimes we are not wise enough with our own tendency to sin. We need to be aware of our ability to hurt, and we need to deal with our sinful tendencies that often come from our own unresolved issues. When we acknowledge these failings, we can begin to find ways to revamp the unhealthy areas of our lives. When we reach for help, healing is possible.

We want to have a capacity to give to others something of the grace of God. We do this by facing our own inadequacies and bringing them to God. How blessed we are to have a God who transforms, who uses even our children to mold us into his likeness. We praise and honor him for the journey of parenting and the blessings it pours out on us.

Postscript

We end with a summary report from the many people who were kind enough to fill out our questionnaires on parenting. We know you will benefit from their words of wisdom and experience.

Most Joyful Experiences:

Watching my children be compassionate and caring for others
Hearing them pray
Having a close relationship with them
Seeing them have a close relationship with God
The return of their love and trust to me
Seeing spiritual, mental, and emotional maturity develop
Observing my children develop a joy in accomplishment
The strength of my family ties with my husband and children
Too many to mention!

Peace in the family
Loving my kids and watching their gifts develop
Our children love the Lord and each other
Seeing them enjoy each other
Seeing them get along and laughing together as a family
Witnessing their faith

Most Painful Experiences:

When they rebelled against God
Watching my children struggle emotionally and behaviorally
Not knowing what to do when children are frustrated
Ignoring our advice
Seeing the hurt my words/actions have on them
Disagreements with spouse regarding family goals and procedures
Dealing with my ADD child
Dishonesty—I hate it!
My own mistakes in parenting
When they come home with hurt feelings from being left out/teased/
    losing out on some event
Having them leave home—it's never the same again

Biggest Personal Struggle:

Being consistent
Controlling my own anger
Parenting during times of family crisis
Frustration and anger that lead to harsh words that hurt my child's
    heart
Isolation and boredom
Not being able to give my children what they wanted
Rebuilding trust after it was broken
Taking care of myself
How to have balance in my own life so I can be a positive role model
How to keep going when I am tired and see little progress in child's
    behavior
One child was very different from the others; I had a hard time know-
    ing how to best parent him

Delegating responsibility
Spending enough time with my children

Advice for Readers:

PRAY!
Talk to other parents with similar values and same-age children
Get support of others so you can discuss your feelings/frustrations
  about parenting
Eat meals together
Be interested in your children's activities
Do things together even through adolescence into adulthood
Give yourself (time, energy, skills) to your children; minimize giving
  things
Try to see the world through the children's eyes
Put child's emotions before yours
Always forgive
Keep a sense of humor
Allow your children to be part of your life
Eat, work, and play together
Don't let them date before sixteen
Be consistent
Balance love and discipline
Don't give up when you're tired
Hand your children over to the care of the Lord
Hold your children often
Rally around God's Word
Be honest
Our children really belong to God—we are merely privileged to care
  for them

Appendix 1

Relationship-Empowerment Parenting Inventory

The purpose of this inventory is to assist you in assessing yourself as a parent. The inventory consists of three parts, corresponding with each of the first three chapters. The first part allows you to understand your style of parenting. Part 2 yields insight into how close your parenting corresponds to biblical principles of parenting. In part 3 we utilize the empowering curve as presented in chapter 3, to enable you to reflect on how well you empower your child. The task of answering and tallying your answers should take no longer than fifteen minutes. At the end of each of the three parts of the inventory, you will find suggestions on how to interpret the results. Taken together, we believe completing this inventory may assist you in gaining needed insights into your parenting approach.

Part 1: Identifying Your Parental Style

Below you will find twenty statements meant to assess your parenting style. Choose the one response from the following four categories that best represents your view of yourself as a parent. For example, if your response to the first statement is "Agree," simply write a 3 in the blank at the beginning of statement one.

(1) Strongly Disagree   (2) Disagree   (3) Agree   (4) Strongly Agree

_____ 1. When my child asks a "why" question, I take the time to explain.
_____ 2. As a parent, my actions speak louder than my words.

_____ 3. I point out strengths I see in my child.

_____ 4. I set clear guidelines for my child.

_____ 5. I feel comfortable teaching skills to my child.

_____ 6. I like to show my child how to do things.

_____ 7. I often give words of encouragement to my child.

_____ 8. I provide the needed structure that allows my child to succeed.

_____ 9. I am able to give clear instructions to my child.

_____10. I'd be glad to have my child follow my example.

_____11. I am there to cheer my child on at school events.

_____12. I'm able to "pull back" and let my child complete a task.

_____13. I explain my religious beliefs and values to my child.

_____14. My child learns best by watching me.

_____15. I'm very supportive of my child.

_____16. I challenge my child to try new things.

_____17. I like to help my child understand his or her world.

_____18. I'm good at demonstrating things to my child.

_____19. I look for opportunities to affirm my child.

_____20. I use my strengths to build up my child.

Scoring Guide

From the above set of responses, simply add together the scores for each of the following:

Content:

Add scores for items 1, 5, 9, 13, 17 ____+____+____+____+____= _____

Action:

Add scores for items 2, 6, 10, 14, 18 ____+____+____+____+____= _____

Relationship:

Add scores for items 3, 7, 11, 15, 19 ____+____+____+____+____= _____

Guidance:

Add scores for items 4, 8, 12, 16, 20 ____+____+____+____+____= _____

Next, add each of the above summary scores together for the
Comprehensive Parenting Competency Score = _____

Finding Your Instrumental and Social-Emotional Parenting Styles

Based on your total score on the Content and Action dimensions, find the approximate point in the table below that represents your style of Instrumental Parenting. You do this by circling the number from top to bottom representing your score on Content, and the number from left to right representing your score on Action. Next, find the point at which the two scores intersect. For example, if your score on Content is 16 and your score on Action is 17, then you have an Empowering instrumental parenting style. Next, use your score on Relationship and Guidance to find your style on the Social-Emotional Parenting table.

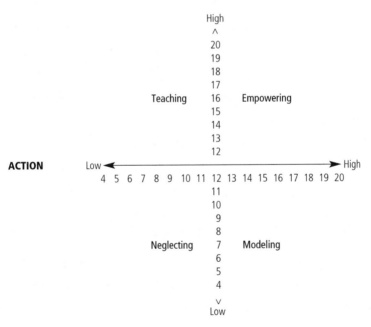

Instrumental Parenting

CONTENT

Social-Emotional Parenting

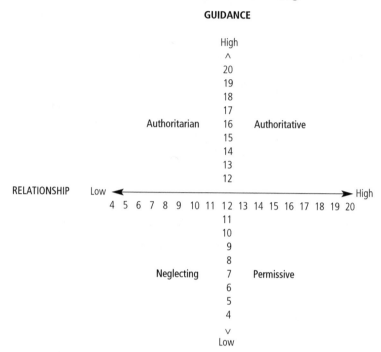

GUIDANCE

High
∧
20
19
18
17

Authoritarian   16   Authoritative
15
14
13
12

RELATIONSHIP   Low ◄─────────────────────────────────► High
4 5 6 7 8 9 10 11 12 13 14 15 16 17 18 19 20
11
10
9
8
Neglecting   7   Permissive
6
5
4
∨
Low

Processing

After identifying your own instrumental and social-emotional parenting styles, did you find any surprises? What are your strengths and what are your limitations in regards to each style? You might want to compare your results with those of your spouse and discuss ways in which you are similar or dissimilar as parents. If your styles are different, do they complement or compete with each other? Can you identify ways in which you and your spouse can grow stronger in either the instrumental or social-emotional style of parenting?

Part 2: Biblical Parental Relationship

Part 2 allows you to assess yourself in regards to the biblical model of parenting as presented in chapter 2. Specifically, this part of the inventory will help you gain insight on the degree to which your parenting is characterized by Commitment, Grace, Empowerment, and Intimacy.

Following are a series of statements about how you feel about your relationship with your children. Choose the one response from the following five categories that best represents your assessment of your relationship as a father or mother with your children. For example, if your response to the first statement is "Sometimes," simply write a 3 in the blank at the beginning of statement 1.

(1) Almost Never   (2) Once in a While   (3) Sometimes   (4) Frequently
(5) Almost Always

___ 1. My love is based upon my child doing what I want him or her to do.
___ 2. When my child makes a mistake, I am able to forgive him or her.
___ 3. I use power to control my child.
___ 4. I freely talk to my child about anything.
___ 5. My child and I make sure we get as much love as we give to each other.
___ 6. My child and I accept each other for who we are.
___ 7. I am unreliable in my actions toward my child.
___ 8. When I feel love toward my child, I verbally express it.
___ 9. My child must be perfect to be acceptable to me.
___ 10. I do what is best for my child.
___ 11. I don't express the emotions I feel for my child.
___ 12. My child can rely on me.
___ 13. When things go wrong, I blame my child.
___ 14. No matter what happens, I will always love my child.
___ 15. I keep secrets from my child.
___ 16. I encourage and build up my child.
___ 17. I question the depth of my love for my child.
___ 18. When my child fails me, I forgive him or her.
___ 19. I am overly dependent on my child.
___ 20. I share my deepest fears and greatest hopes with my child.
___ 21. I express love to get what I want from my child.
___ 22. I accept my child's differences.
___ 23. My child cannot count on me to be there for him or her.
___ 24. When I feel angry toward my child, I verbally express it.
___ 25. I feel ashamed of my child.
___ 26. I want what is best for my child and give of myself to make it happen.
___ 27. I keep my inner feelings to myself.
___ 28. There is constancy in my relationship with my child.
___ 29. I blame my child during times of trouble.
___ 30. I am committed to my child for better or worse.

___ 31. I avoid talking about controversial things with my child.

___ 32. I use my strengths and resources to equip my child.

Finding Your Score on the Biblical Parenting Model

Write the score you gave in response to each statement in the appropriate box below.

Add up each column, adding (+) or subtracting (-) each score as indicated by the +/- symbol.

Commitment			Grace			Empowerment			Intimacy		
Q#	+/-	Your Score	Q#	+/-	Your Score	Q#	+/-	Your Score	Q#	+/-	Your Score
1	-		2	+		3	-		4	+	
5	-		6	+		7	-		8	+	
10	+		9	-		12	+		11	-	
14	+		13	-		16	+		15	-	
17	-		18	+		19	-		20	+	
21	-		22	+		23	-		24	+	
26	+		25	-		28	+		27	-	
30	+		29	-		32	+		31	-	
TOTAL			TOTAL			TOTAL			TOTAL		

Add your four total scores for your grand total biblical parenting score and record your scores on the continuums on the next page.

Processing

There are a number of ways in which you can use the results to help you understand yourself as a parent. You might begin by comparing your score for each of the four dimensions. Since we have found a fairly strong correlation between the four dimensions of parenting, take note if your score on one is significantly lower than the others. You also might compare your scores with those of your spouse, using the results to discuss ways in which you each relate to your child and how you might do it differently.

Part 3: Mastering the Maturity-Empowerment Curve

Figure 3.1 illustrates a maturity-empowerment curve that is based on the principle that parents need to adjust their mode of interaction to fit the age and maturity of their child. Assess your competency for each of the following modes of interacting with your child. Refer to chapter 3

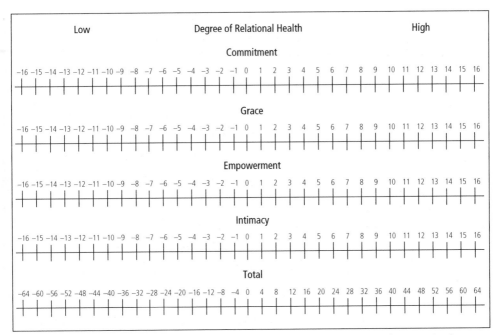

Scores on Commitment, Grace, Empowerment, and Intimacy range from −4 and +16. Scores between −4 and +4 can be considered to be in the average range. Scores beyond this in the minus direction can be considered low and scores in the plus direction high. A score between −16 and + 16 in the grand total biblical parenting scale can be considered average.

if you need a reminder of the Telling, Teaching, Modeling, and Delegating modes.

Below you will find twenty statements to help you assess your parenting strength on each of these dimensions. (Since these dimensions overlap some with *styles of parenting,* you will find some of the items below to be identical to those you responded to on pages 191–92.) Choose the one response from the following four categories that best represents how you view yourself as a parent. For example, if your response to the first statement is "Agree," simply write a 3 in the blank at the beginning of statement 1.

(1) Strongly Disagree   (2) Disagree   (3) Agree   (4) Strongly Agree

____ 1. When my child asks a "why" question, I take the time to explain.
____ 2. As a parent, my actions speak louder than my words.
____ 3. I'm effective in communicating with my child.
____ 4. I always let my child finish a task when he or she is ready.

___ 5. I feel comfortable teaching skills to my child.
___ 6. I feel comfortable showing my child how to do things.
___ 7. I tell my child what is expected of him or her.
___ 8. I'm always ready to give up control over my child when the time is right.
___ 9. I'm good at giving instructions to my child.
___ 10. I'd be glad to have my child follow my example.
___ 11. I set clear guidelines for my child.
___ 12. I am good at "pulling back" and letting my child complete a task.
___ 13. I'm good at explaining religious beliefs to my child.
___ 14. My child can learn best by watching me.
___ 15. My child knows what I expect of him or her.
___ 16. I challenge my child to try to do things on their own.
___ 17. I'm good at helping my child understand their world.
___ 18. I'm good at demonstrating things to my child.
___ 19. I set clear rules and boundaries for my child.
___ 20. I look for opportunities to let my child take over responsibility for a task.

Scoring Guide

From the above set of responses, simply add together the scores for each of the following:

Telling:
     Add scores for items 3, 7, 11, 15, 19 ___+___+___+___+___=___

Teaching:
     Add scores for items 1, 5, 9, 13, 17 ___+___+___+___+___=___

Modeling:
     Add scores for items 2, 6, 10, 14, 18 ___+___+___+___+___=___

Delegating:
     Add scores for items 4, 8, 12, 16, 20 ___+___+___+___+___=___

Processing

After you have completed this assessment, note differences between your four scores. Which area of parenting do you see as your strength? Telling, teaching, modeling, or delegating? Why does that area come easily to you? Which area is your weakness? What makes it difficult for you? How could you be empowered in this area? Next, share results with your spouse and together discuss the ways in which each of you might strengthen each mode of parenting.

If you feel it is appropriate, ask your children how they perceive each of your four modes of parenting. (In doing this you need to be "age appropriate" in your conversation. Younger children may not be able to comprehend distinctions between telling and teaching.) Children at most ages will be able to tell us if they think we explain things in a helpful way. Although children at all ages are aware of how we live out what we say (modeling), our teenage children are probably the ones who are the quickest to point out our deficits in this area. When they do, you might think of concrete ways in which you can be more congruent. Age appropriateness may especially be true in discussing issues of delegating. So ask a younger child, "Does Mommy or Daddy let you do things for yourself, or do they do it for you even when you can do it for yourself?" Older children will probably accuse you of not delegating responsibilities soon enough. This opens up a discussion of why you might hesitate to delegate responsibility or why they wish you would give them more responsibility.

Appendix 2
Recommended Reading List

Adoption

Eldridge, S. (1999). *Jewels among jewels: 20 things adoptive children wish their parents knew.* New York: Dell Publishing.

Gray, D. (2002). *Attaching in adoption.* Indianapolis: Perspectives Press.

Bonding

Karen, R. (1998). *Becoming attached.* New York: Oxford University Press.

Coparenting

Deutsch, F. (1999). *Halving it all: How equally shared parenting works.* Cambridge: Harvard University Press.

Eating Disorders

Chernin, K. (1994). *The obsession: Reflections on the tyranny of slenderness.* New York: Harper Perennial.

Roth, G. (1992). *When food is love: Exploring the relationship between eating and intimacy.* New York: Plume.

General Family

Elkind, D. (1996). *Ties that stress: The new family imbalance.* Cambridge: Harvard University Press.

Balswick, J., & Balswick, J. K. (1997). *Families in pain: Working through the hurts.* Grand Rapids: Revell.

Balswick, J., & Balswick, J. K. (1999). *The family: A Christian perspective on the contemporary home.* Grand Rapids: Baker.

General Parenting

Hamner, T., & Turner, P. (1990). *Parenting in contemporary society.* Needham Heights, MA: Allyn & Bacon.

MacKenzie, R. (2001). *Setting limits with your strong-willed child: Eliminate conflict by establishing clear, firm, and respectful boundaries.* Roseville, CA: Prima Publishing.

McMinn, L. (2000). *Growing strong daughters: Encouraging girls to become all they're meant to be.* Grand Rapids: Baker.

Scott, B. (1989). *Relief for hurting parents: What to do and how to think when you're having trouble with your kids.* Nashville: Thomas Nelson.

Later-Life Families

Piper, B., & Balswick, J. K. (1997). *Then they leave home: Parenting after the kids grow up.* Downers Grove, IL: InterVarsity Press.

Premature Babies

Linden, D. W., Paroli, E. T., & Doron, M. W. (2000). *Preemies: The essential guide for parents of premature babies.* New York: Pocket Books.

Sexual Development and Behavior

Johnson, T. C. (1999). *Understanding your child's sexual behavior: What's natural and healthy.* Oakland: New Harbinger Publication.

Sibling Relationships

Bank, S., & Kahn, M. (1982). *The sibling bond.* New York: Basic Books.

Single-Parent Families

Weiss, R. (1979). *Going it alone: The family life and social situation of the single parent.* New York: Basic Books.

Step-parenting/Blended Families

Papernow, P. (1993). *Becoming a stepfamily.* San Francisco: Jossey-Bass Inc.
Visher, E. B., & Visher, J. S. (1988). *Old loyalties, new ties.* New York: Brunner/Mazel.

Teenage Children

Campbell, R. (1993). *How to really love your teenager.* Colorado Springs: Chariot Victor.
Cline, F., & Fay, J. (1992). *Parenting teens with love and logic.* Colorado Springs: Pinon Press.
Gould, S. (1997). *Teenagers: The continuing challenge.* New York: Hawthorne Books.
Kindlon, D., & Thompson, M. (2000). *Raising Cain: Protecting the emotional life of boys.* New York: Ballantine Books.
Kurcinka, M. (2000). *Kids, parents, and power struggles: Winning for a lifetime.* New York: HarperCollins.
Pipher, M. (1994). *Reviving Ophelia: Saving the selves of adolescent girls.* New York: Ballantine Books.

Young Children

Campbell, R. (1992). *How to really love your child.* Colorado Springs: Chariot Victor.
Dreikurs, R. (1992). *The challenge of parenthood.* New York: Plume.
Dinkmeyer, D., & McKay, G. (1973). *Raising a responsible child: Practical steps to successful family relationships.* New York: Simon & Schuster.
Glennon, W. (2000). *200 ways to raise a boy's emotional intelligence.* Berkeley: Conari Press.
Keirsey, D., & Bates, M. (1984). *Please understand me.* Del Mar, CA: Prometheus Nemesis Book Co.
MacKenzie, R. (1998). *Setting limits: How to raise responsible, independent children by providing clear boundaries.* Rocklin, CA: Prima Publishing.
Sears, W., & Sears, M. (2001). *Attachment parenting book: A commonsense guide to understanding and nurturing your baby.* Boston: Little, Brown.
Sears, W., & Sears, M. (1996). *Parenting the fussy baby and the high-need child: Everything you need to know—from birth to age five.* Boston: Little, Brown.

References

Ainsworth, M. (1978). *Patterns of attachment: A psychological study of the strange situation.* New York: Halsted Press.

Anderson, H., & Mitchell, K. (1983). *Leaving home.* Louisville: Westminster John Knox.

Baumrind, D. (1996). The discipline controversy revisited. *Family Relations, 45,* 405–15.

Blankenshorn, D. (1995). *Fatherless America.* New York: Basic Books.

Bowlby, J. (1979). *The making and breaking of affectional bonds.* London: Tavistock.

Buechner, F. (1980). *Godric.* San Francisco: HarperCollins.

Buechner, F. (1982). *The sacred journey.* San Francisco: Harper & Row.

Burtchaell, J. T. (1985). *For better, for worse.* In Rodney Clapp (1993). *Families at the crossroads.* Downers Grove, IL: InterVarsity Press.

Chilman, C. (1980, November). Social and psychological research concerning adolescent child-bearing: 1970–1980. *Journal of Marriage and the Family,* 793–805.

Dinkmeyer, D., & McKay, G. (1976). *Systematic training for effective parenting (STEP).* Circle Pines, MN: American Guidance Service.

Dreikurs, R., & Scholtz, V. (1958). *Children: The challenge.* New York: Hawthorn Books.

Ehrensaft, D. (1990). *Parenting together: Men and women sharing the care of their children.* Urbana: University of Illinois Press.

Erikson, E. (1963). *Childhood and society.* New York: Norton.

Fein, R. A. (1978). Research in fathering: Social policy and an emergent perspective. *Journal of Social Issues, 34* (1), 122–36.

Henry, C., & Peterson, G. (1995). Adolescent social competence, parental qualities, and parental satisfaction. *American Journal of Orthopsychiatry, 65*(2), 249–62.

Karen, R. (1998). *Becoming attached.* New York: Oxford University Press.

Keillor, G. (1994). *Leaving home: A collection of Lake Wobegon stories.* Harrisonburg, VA: Donnelley & Sons.

Kluger, J., & Park, A. (2001, April 30). The quest for the super kid. *Time.*

Maccoby, E. (1980). *Social development: Psychological growth and the parent-child relationship.* New York: Harcourt Brace Jovanovich.

Naylor, A. (1970). Some determinants of parent-infant relationships. In L. Dittman (Ed.). (1970). *What we can learn from infants.* Washington, DC: National Association for the Education of Young Children.

Nouwen, H. (1984, May/June). Intimacy, fecundity and ecstasy. *Radix Magazine,* 8–11.

Rivers, F. (1998). *The last sin eater.* Wheaton: Tyndale House.

Russell, G. (1978). The father role and its relation to masculinity, femininity, and androg-
    yny. *Child Development, 49,* 1174–81.

Saint-Exupery, A. (1943). *Little prince.* New York: Harcourt, Brace & World.

Smalley, G., & Trent, J. (1986). *The blessing.* Nashville: Thomas Nelson.

Sroufe, L. A. (2000). Early relationships and the development of children. *Infant Mental
    Health Journal, 21* (1/2), 67–74.

Viorst, J. (1986). *Necessary losses.* New York: Fawcett Gold Medal.

Walters, J., & Walters, L. (1980, November). Parent-child relationships: A review,
    1970–1979. *Journal of Marriage and the Family,* 807–22.

Jack and Judy Balswick teach at Fuller Theological Seminary in Pasadena, California. Judy, a licensed marriage and family therapist, teaches family therapy and supervises courses in marital and family therapy; Jack instructs family ministry, child development, and cross-cultural courses. **Boni Piper** is a full-time marital and family therapist, and **Don Piper** is a pastor with thirty years of ministry service. Don and Boni live in Seattle, Washington.